Secrets Of The Negro Baseball League

To order additional copies, please contact us.
BookSurge, LLC
www.booksurge.com
1-866-308-6235
orders@booksurge.com

WRITTEN BY
L.G. MARTINEZ

SECRETS OF THE NEGRO BASEBALL LEAGUE

As Told By Dennis Biddle

2005

Secrets Of The Negro Baseball League

No one knows the whole truth. Not all of it. Only Sherwood Brewer and I were there when it all happened. We watched the wrongs being done and we fought the conspiracies as they unfolded. We fought the very organizations that claimed to represent us, and we uncovered what no one wanted us to find.

Thank God we weren't too late. Or were we?

There are a lot of misconceptions when it comes to the Negro Leagues and what happened to those who played. This book is intended to educate the world, to tell the truth before it is swept under the rug and lost forever. Although Sherwood Brewer passed on before we had a chance to publish this book, I will continue to educate the public in any way I can until the truth be known by everyone.

INTRODUCTION

The first Negro League was started in 1920 because *men of color* were not permitted the opportunity of playing in the Major League due to the infamous *'gentlemen's agreement.'* The gentlemen's agreement came from a Congressional ruling *"The Jim Crow,"* used by major league owners to keep men of color from playing on their Major League teams. This agreement prevailed for forty-seven (47) years until the Brooklyn Dodgers signed Jackie Robinson in 1947. With the walls slowly falling, more blacks were admitted into the Major Leagues, and in 1960, the Negro Baseball League ended.

Dennis "Bose" Biddle was born in Magnolia, Arkansas on June 24, 1935.

On February 27, 1996, he was read into the Congressional Record as the youngest player to join the Negro Baseball League at the age of seventeen. Dennis has been awarded a Lifetime Achievement Award from the Old Time Ballplayers Association of Wisconsin and has earned a place in their Hall of Fame. He is also the president of Yesterday's Negro League Baseball Players Foundation, the only organization that represents all the living players from the Negro Baseball League.

If you played in the Negro League and need assistance, please call Yesterday's Negro League Baseball Player's Foundation.

If you would like to make a donation, please call or write:

Yesterday's Negro League Baseball Players Foundation
9418 North Green Bay Road
Suite 124 Milwaukee, WI 53209
(414) 355-2075

CHAPTER ONE
A Reunion

I stood on the dry, faded grass of the infield with hundreds of men and two women. I was amazed as I looked over the multitude of people on the field. My heart pounded with excitement. I was awestruck while the cameras flashed tirelessly. As we stood there representing a past that had seemed to be long forgotten, I felt immense pride knowing that I had been part of this remarkable history and I reflected back on what had brought me to this day.

I was only seventeen-years-old when I signed a contract to play for the Chicago American Giants, a Negro League baseball team, back in 1953. I had pitched seven no-hitters in high school and my coach thought for sure the major leagues would take me as a first round draft pick, so I anxiously waited by the telephone with immense anticipation that day just before my high school graduation. The day was long, but the major leagues never called.

I was devastated because I loved baseball. I played ball ever since I was a child. As young as six, you could find me in the dusty streets of the small town called Magnolia, Arkansas, playing stickball with my brothers and cousins. We used an old broomstick and a tennis ball, and that's how I learned to hit and pitch. I practiced throwing the tennis ball every day until I became a decent pitcher.

When I was twelve-years-old, I finally got the opportunity to play with a real baseball. I found it in a box. I'll never forget the day I saw *the box*. It was in early spring in 1947, just after Jackie Robinson was accepted into the major leagues and baseball was the talk of the town. We all idolized Jackie Robinson. We all wanted to be like him. Unfortunately, we didn't have baseballs or bats or gloves to play baseball, so we improvised with our stickball games. The black schools in our area were in the beginning stages of organizing baseball teams, and our coach wanted to organize a team for our school too.

Since everything was segregated back then, I went to an all-Black school on one side of town and Whites went to the all-White school on the other side of town. Our school would get all the hand-me-downs from the white school across town. That's how our school got books and materials and sporting equipment for us to use. I guess it bothered some, but for me it was OK. It was just the way life was for us back then.

Every day after school the other boys and I would go to the open gym to play basketball or throw the football around. One day I was coming down the hallway, when I saw three boxes outside the gym door. They were hand-me-downs from the White school. Two of the boxes had piles of books in them. The other box was the one that caught my eye. A boy named Bo Dunn was with me and we both saw the box at the same time. It was full of sports equipment and we saw bats and baseball gloves sticking out the top of it, so we quickly ran over to the box. I grabbed a five-fingered baseball glove, Bo grabbed a catcher's mitt and we each grabbed a baseball. I was elated! I didn't care if they were hand-me-downs as long as I could play real baseball. It was like a dream come true. I was holding something I never thought I would ever be able to have. I felt like it was Christmas and these were our gifts! Right away we started throwing the ball to each other. I threw straight into his glove. It felt so natural.

Every day, for several hours after school, we would throw the baseball in the school yard. I eventually developed a curveball to go with my already-intimidating fastball. Kids would stand by and watch us throw to each other. Sometimes other kids would throw to each other too. During lunch break someone would get a bat and kids would all line up and try to hit my curveball. We didn't think much about how badly Bo would have gotten hurt had someone foul tipped a ball back at him until we actually started practicing as a team. The coach came up with a facemask for Bo to wear while we practiced. We soon realized how important it was. He got foul tipped in the face several times during practice!

Bo was great. He was the only player on the team that could catch my curveball. He and I would practice for hours and hours everyday, pitching and catching. We practiced every day after school as a team too, and soon I developed a drop pitch (today it's called a sinker or a split-finger) that no one could hit.

We played high school ball once a week. During the first game that was played between the Black schools, the opposing team shared their newer catcher's mitt and chest protector with us. We, in turn, shared our catcher's mitt and facemask with other teams we played against too. No team had everything, so we shared what equipment we had. That's just how it was.

I struck out fifteen players from their team that day and pitched my first no-hitter. The schools that we played against had two or three players that really played well. Over the three years that I played in high school, I got better and better. So did the teams we played against, but there was still no school that could beat us. By that time I had perfected my curve ball. When a kid standing with a bat saw the ball coming straight at him, he'd instinctively step away. Then the ball would curve away from him at the last moment, and go right over the plate. He had no idea what had happened.

Word got around about my pitching and pretty soon the local Black men's team asked Bo Dunn and me to play with them on the Sundays that they played. I was asked to pitch and Bo Dunn was asked to catch for them. The manager said he would pay me seventy-five cents for each game I pitched. Wow! I was going to get paid to do what I loved. I thought this was great, so I accepted!

When Sunday came, my parents left the house to get to church. They were very religious and kept the Lord in our daily lives. They were both Sunday school teachers so they left early every Sunday and I met them at church later. I waited awhile and then, instead of going to Sunday school, I walked over to the park. I got there sometime after 10:00 am to get my uniform and practice. I remember they gave me a uniform that was too big for me and it was mismatched. My pants were a different color than my jersey. My number was thirty-three. That became the number I used throughout high school and in the Negro Leagues.

In the first inning I had struck out two of the men I faced. I was feeling proud (and happy that I was going to get seventy-five cents too). The game was zero/zero in the third inning. I was standing on the mound, ready to set up my pitch, when I saw my dad walking up. My heart sunk as he walked across the field and came right up to me on the pitching mound and said, "Come on, you're coming with me."

I was never so embarrassed in my whole life. Bo Dunn was my catcher and his dad didn't come after him. My dad told the manager I couldn't play with them anymore. As we walked home from the ballpark my dad told me the Lord should come first in my life, not baseball.

I took the uniform back to the manager the next day and was looking forward to my seventy-five cents but the manager said I had to pitch at least five innings to get paid, so I never got paid, or punished, for skipping church or Sunday school that day to play ball.

But the very next week I was there again. This time we went in a car and drove out of town and played ball against another team from another town. This time I got my seventy-five cents. I continued to sneak out on the Sunday's that the men's team played. I got yelled at on a regular basis for it, but I think my dad (and mom) realized I wasn't going to quit playing ball, so after awhile they stopped harassing me.

I was quite athletic in high school. I was on the football, basketball, track and baseball teams. In the fall, I played football. I was the high school team's quarterback. Back then, we played offense and defense so I was the kicker on the team too. After football season ended, I played basketball during the winter. Then, come spring, it was baseball season. I played baseball and ran track in the spring and summer months. I lettered in all four sports but baseball was by far my favorite.

During my senior year I received scholarship offers from three different colleges. Two scholarship offers were to play basketball and one offer was to play football for Coach Eddie Robinson at Grambling College. That offer interested me the most, so I visited the campus. I roomed with another boy who was being recruited to Grambling College for football. His name was Willie Davis, who later became a professional football player and is now in the Hall of Fame. It was interesting that I was chosen to room with Willie Davis because we had played football against each other during high school. Willie and I talked about that game and we laughed about it too because it was a joke of a game. Our team played against the Texarkana Lions, Davis' high school team. We lost fifty-five to nothing. I was the quarterback and Willie was the defensive end. I could never even get set to throw the ball because every time I turned around, Willie was all over me. He tackled me over and over, and every time he tackled me he would stand up over me, and sing, "Have mercy Mrs. Percy, did I get him?" Then he would smile and run off.

There were no hard feelings about it. They were a much more experienced team and they were better than we were. They were better than everybody that year. They won the state championship among Black schools that year.

The next day we had a breakfast at the college, and coach Robinson approached me. He must have heard about my baseball abilities because he said to me, "Hey kid, I hear you want to be a professional baseball player."

I said, "I love baseball. One day I hope to play professional."

He replied, "Kid, if baseball is your love, you should stick with it."

He also told me they had a baseball team but there wasn't a scholarship available for baseball. That's all that was said about the subject.

The other scholarship offers I received were both for basketball. One scholarship offered was for Arkansas AM&N, which is now the University of Arkansas, and the other was for Philander Smith College in Little Rock, Arkansas. No one, however, offered me a scholarship to play baseball. I decided to talk it over with my high school coach to see if he had any advice. He told me he heard that Blacks were being drafted right into the major leagues now, and with my ability I could be a number one draft pick for the major leagues. With that information, I decided to concentrate on my ballgame and be the number one draft pick, for sure. I practiced and played and sweat for baseball, preparing myself, and hoping a Major league scout might see me play.

The Major league draft was the Saturday before I graduated from high school. I was excited and ready for the call to join the major leagues. I eagerly sat by the telephone waiting for the call. I sat there all day but the telephone never rang. My mother used to talk about the look on my face as I waited by the telephone. I don't remember ever being so disappointed in my young life.

I graduated the next day. It was a sunny Sunday afternoon in May of 1953. It was supposed to be an exciting and fun-filled day but I felt very sad and alone. I was seventeen-years-old and I was getting ready to part from friends I had known all my life. I felt like I might never see them again. It was also deflating that the major leagues had not called me. I felt like I had somehow failed. After the graduation ceremony, I made up my mind that I would accept the scholarship offer from Coach Eddie Robinson and I was resigned to the fact that I was going to play football for Grambling College the next fall. I came to the conclusion that Grambling was a good college and I would be getting a free college education. I liked football too, so I wouldn't mind playing for them.

I still felt lost and empty, though. For a few days I wandered around wondering what I was going to do with myself for the summer. I spent some time with my friends and contemplated what kind of summer job I should get. The week seemed to drag slowly by.

The following Sunday morning as I was getting ready to leave the house for Sunday school, the telephone rang. I didn't think much of it when I heard it ring. I was just getting ready to go out the door. I answered it and the voice on the other end asked, "Is this Dennis Biddle, the baseball player?"

I said, "Yes."

The voice on the other end said, "I've watched you play ball. You're pretty good. How would like to play for the Chicago American Giants in the Negro League? You'll get paid."

I said, "I would love to."

I had no idea what the Negro League was. I just figured the person on the other end of the line was the manager of a local team and that I would be playing ball in my own hometown and being paid to play.

Then he said, "You have a try out in Chicago. Tuesday morning, eleven o'clock. Washington Park, diamond number seven."

"Okay," I agreed, and I hung up the phone.

A thousand thoughts seemed to race through my mind. For a split second I was excited. I was just invited to try out for the Chicago American Giants by a talent scout. Then I was confused. Who were the Chicago American Giants? Where and when had he seen me play? What was the Negro League he mentioned?

But then reality quickly settled in. Who was he kidding? There was no way I could afford to get to Chicago, especially not in two days! I had no money to get to Chicago.

I thought a lot about the call as I walked over to the church. I talked to my mom about it when I saw her. I told her I wanted to go to Chicago but I knew I couldn't because I didn't have the money to get there.

After church I called the bus station just to see how much it would cost to get from Magnolia to Chicago. I didn't have high hopes of getting there but I felt I should at least find out how much it would cost. They told me it would be fourteen dollars one way. I went home and told my parents what I had found out. We discussed the situation as a family. We talked about the fact that we didn't have any money and that I didn't know anyone in the city. I was hopeful, but deep down I knew it was impossible to get there for the try out. Besides, I had already made up my mind that I was going to go to Grambling College in the fall.

That evening my mom left the house and I went out on the front porch into the summer night to ponder my future. I was thinking about baseball and wondering what my next move was going to be. I was wondering where I could come up with the money to get to Chicago. My mom didn't say where she was going but when she came back to the house, she quietly came up to me. She handed me a twenty-dollar bill and said, "This is all I could get." She just put it in my hand. I looked at it and I thought, "Wow." For the first time in my life I realized I was getting ready to leave home. I was actually going to able to go and pursue my dream. It was a miracle.

I was in a state of disbelief. The bus to Chicago was the next day at 9:00 am. I had so much to do! I rushed to my room and started looking in my dresser drawers for clothes to take with me and for any loose change. I grabbed my glove and my spikes and a silk shirt that my mom had given me for my high school graduation. I had but one change of clothes in my duffle bag. That was enough.

My dad was still concerned. He came to me and said, "You don't know nobody, son, and it's a big city, Chicago. Don't go. Don't do it."

Then my sister started crying. My brothers started crying out, "Don't go, Dennis."

Everyone was telling me not to go, except my mom. She didn't say a word.

The next morning I woke up and got ready to leave for Chicago. I hugged my sister and brothers. Then as I approached my dad, he started crying. It was the first time I ever saw him cry. "Son," he pleaded, "you don't know nobody in that big city. Please don't go."

I looked over to my mom. She stood quietly by the door with all the confidence in the world in me. She wasn't crying. She was a pillar of strength and reassurance. She just kissed me, gave me a hug and said, "Baby, good luck." I felt that hug all the way to Chicago. I truly did.

I left the house and started toward the bus station. It was my first trip away from home and it would mark the beginning of a journey that would last my lifetime. Since I had to pass by where my grandfather lived, I stopped in to say good-bye. He asked me where I was going. I told him, and then he started crying too and told me not to go. I said, "Grandpa, I gotta go."

I was building more and more courage for this trip with every step I took toward the bus station. I went to my girlfriend's house and she walked me to the bus station. She was crying too. I got on the bus and she sadly waved as the bus pulled away.

For nearly one thousand miles, from Arkansas to Illinois, I thought about my future and how I was going to find Washington Park. I thought about the team I was trying out for and I wondered some more about this League he mentioned. I wondered if it was a professional baseball league. Then I thought again about my mother's hug.

I got to Chicago early Tuesday morning. It must have been about 5:00 am. Here I was, this young country boy in the big city of Chicago, Illinois. The first thing I remember seeing was an escalator that led up to the street from the bus station. I had never seen an escalator before. I called them rolling steps and I was afraid to get on them, so I used the traditional stairs. As I stepped out the doorway onto the streets of Chicago, I saw a lot of tall buildings. It was quite a sight for me. We only had one or two tall buildings in Magnolia and they were only two stories high. These building were magnificent. They actually seemed to touch the sky. I guess that's why they called them skyscrapers. They had to be at least twenty stories high! I had only heard about them before and now here I was, staring up into the sky at them, in person.

After a moment of awe, I looked over and saw a bus that had stopped at a red light on the corner of Randolph and Clark so I waked over and I asked the bus driver how to get to Washington Park. He told me I would have to ride this bus for a short time and then transfer. I had only my duffle bag and five dollars and some change left. I paid the bus driver fifty-five cents for the bus fare and got on the bus. Looking back on that day, it never occurred to me how I would get home if I didn't make the team.

He told me when to get off and what bus I was to transfer to next. I got off and waited for the right bus and when it came, I got on that bus and again I asked the bus driver how to get to Washington Park. The bus driver said, "I'll call out the street number and when I call out South Parkway, now King Drive, you get off and walk across the street and that's Washington Park."

When he called out South Parkway, I got off the bus and stood on the corner of 51st and South Parkway. I stood for a moment and felt the calm breeze in my face and then I walked across the street. I was at peace. I couldn't wait to get to the park because I knew I could play ball well. I wasn't afraid of failing, I just didn't know how to get where I needed to be to try out for the team.

I walked down 51st Street and passed a large apartment building. The address on the front read 620 East 51st Street. I approached a man who was sitting there and asked him if he knew where Washington Park, diamond number seven was. He pointed across the street and told me that was Washington Park and that I would have to go over there to the park and look for diamond number seven. Innocently, I asked him if I could leave my bag with him, and he said, "Sure. You can leave your bag."

I took my glove and my spikes out of my duffle bag. Then, being a seventeen-year-old country boy, I gave the big city man my duffle bag with all of my belongings in it and I walked across the street to the park.

I glanced around the park and coincidently, the first diamond I saw read diamond number seven. No one was there yet. It was early and I didn't have to be there for a long time. After what seemed to be an hour or more, people started straggling in. We all started throwing the ball around. I was very comfortable with the guys and throwing the ball back and forth. It was like the times I played catch in high school with Bo.

Then a man came on the field and introduced himself as Frank Crawford. "I'm the owner of the Chicago American Giants and you are here to try out for the team," he said to me.

The other guys on the field already played for the Giants so I was the only one trying out that day. It was a regularly scheduled practice for the team so we threw the ball around and then I pitched batting practice. After that we had infield practice.

Then Mr. Crawford walked up to me and said he had some papers he wanted me to sign. It was a contract to play for the Giants. It had already been typed out with my name on it and everything. It was a four-year binding contract to play for the Chicago American Giants in the Negro Baseball League. It stated that I was going to get paid five hundred dollars every month to play baseball for them. I was delighted by the proposal and I signed the contract. My dream was going to come true! I was going to be a professional baseball player!

Negro National League of Professional Baseball Clubs

Uniform Player's Contract

Parties

The CHICAGO AMERICAN GIANTS

herein called the Club, and DENNIS BIDDLE

of 627 DORSE ST. MAGNOLIA, ARKANSAS.   herein called the Player.

Recital

The Club is a member of the Negro National League of Professional Baseball Clubs. As such, and jointly with the other members of the League, it is a party to the Negro National League Constitution and to agreements and rules with the Negro American League of Professional Baseball Clubs and its constituent clubs. The purpose of these agreements and rules is to insure to the public wholesome and high-class professional baseball by defining the relations between Club and Player, between club and club, and between league and league.

Agreement

In view of the facts above recited the parties agree as follows:

Employment

1. The Club hereby employs the Player to render skilled service as a baseball player in connection with all games of the Club during the year 1953-1954 - 1954-1955 4 YEARS including the Club's training season, the Club's exhibition games, the Club's playing season, any all-star games and the Negro World Series, (or any other official series in which the Club may participate and in any receipts of which the player may be entitled to share); and the Player covenants that he will perform with diligence and fidelity and service stated and such duties as may be required of him in such employment.

Salary

2. For the service aforesaid the Club will pay the Player a salary of

per month from MAY - SEPT EACH YEAR   as follows: $ 500

In semi-monthly installments after the commencement of the playing season on the .... and .... day of each month covered by this contract, unless the Player is "abroad" with the Club for the purpose of playing games, in which event the amount then due shall be paid on the first week-day after the return "home" of the Club, the terms "home" and "abroad" meaning respectively at and away from the city in which the Club has its baseball field.

If the player is in the service of the Club for part of the month only, he shall receive such proportion of the salary above mentioned, as the number of days of his actual employment bears to the number of days in said month.

Loyalty

3. The Player will faithfully serve the Club or any other Club to which, in conformity with the agreements above recited, this contract may be assigned, and pledges himself to the American public to conform to high standards of personal conduct, of fair play and good sportsmanship.

Service

4. (a) The player agrees that, while under contract or reservation, he will not play baseball (except post-season games as hereinafter stated) otherwise than for the Club or a Club assignee hereof; that he will not engage in professional boxing or wrestling; and that, except with the written consent of the Club or its assignee, he will not engage in any game or exhibition of football, basketball, hockey or other athletic sport.

Post-season Games

(b) The Player agrees that, while under contract or reservation, he will not play in any post-season baseball games except in conformity with the Negro Major League Rules, or with or against an ineligible player or team.

Assignment

5. (a) In case of assignment of this contract to another Club, the Player shall promptly report to the assignee club; accrued salary shall be payable when he so reports; and each successive assignee shall become liable to the Player for his salary during his term of service with such assignee, and the Club shall not be liable therefor. If the player fails to report as above specified, he shall not be entitled to salary after the date he receives notice of assignment.

Termination

(b) This contract may be terminated at any time by the Club or by any assignee upon five days' written notice to the Player.

Regulations

6. The Player accepts as part of this contract the Regulations printed on the third page hereof, and also such reasonable modifications of them and such other reasonable regulations as the Club may announce from time to time.

Agreements and Rules

7. The Negro American League Constitution, and the Negro Major League Agreements and Rules and all amendments thereto hereafter adopted, are hereby made a part of this contract, and the Club and Player agree to accept, abide by and comply with the same and all decisions of the League President or Board of Owners, pursuant thereto.

Renewal

8. (a) On or before April 1st (or if Sunday, then the succeeding business day) of the year next following the last playing season covered by this contract, by written notice to the Player at his address following his signature hereto (or if none be given, then at his last address of record with the club), the Club or any assignee hereof may renew this contract for the term of that year except that the salary shall be such as the parties may then agree upon, or in default of agreement the Player will accept such salary rate as the Club may fix, or else will not play baseball otherwise than for the Club or for an assignee hereof.

(b) The Club's right of reservation of the Player, and of renewal of this contract as aforesaid, and the promise of the Player not to play otherwise than with the Club or an assignee hereof, have been taken into consideration in determining the salary specified herein and the undertaking by the Club to pay said salary is the consideration for both said reservation, renewal option and promise, and the Player's service.

Disputes

9. In case of dispute between the Player and the Club or any assignee hereof, the same shall be referred to the League President as an umpire, and his decision shall be accepted by all parties as final, and the Club and the Player agree that any such dispute, or any claim or complaint by either party against the other, shall be presented to the League President within sixty days from the date it arose.

10. This contract is subject to Federal or State legislation, regulations, executive or other official orders, or other governmental action, now or hereafter in effect, respecting Military, Naval, Air or other governmental service, which may, directly or indirectly, affect the Player, the Club or the League; and subject also to all rules, regulations, decisions or other action by the Negro American League or the League President, including the right of the League President to suspend the operation of this contract during any National emergency.

Supplemental Agreements

11. The player expressly covenants and agrees that in the event of his breach of contract the Club shall have the right to apply to any court of competent jurisdiction, domestic or foreign, for an injunction, or for relief, in such manner as shall be deemed necessary.

12. The Club and Player covenant that this contract fully sets forth all understandings and agreements between them, and agree that no other understandings or agreements, whether heretofore or hereafter made, shall be valid, recognizable, or of any effect whatsoever, unless expressly set forth in a new or supplemental contract executed by the Player and the Club (acting through its duly authorized agent) and complying with all agreements and rules to which this contract is subject.

Signed this _____21_____ day of _____May_____ A. D. 195_3_
(SEAL)

Chicago American Giants
(Club)

By _W S Bridgeforth_
(President)

Witness:

Paul Jones

Dennis Biddle
(Player)

Wallace Guthrie
(Home Address of Player)

Mr. Crawford told me he had a place for me to stay and he asked me where my bag was. I told him it was across the street. When we walked across the street to get it, I couldn't remember where I had left it. The man was gone and so was my duffle bag. I was a little confused. Soon, a lady came to the door of the building and asked if I was the boy who left his bag. I said, "Yes."

She said, "Mr. Washington had to go to work and he said that you would be back for it."

I asked her if she knew his telephone number because I wanted to thank him for watching my bag. She gave me my bag and then looked up the telephone number of Mr. Washington and gave that to me as well. Then Mr. Crawford took me to his car and we drove over to 47th and South Parkway to a rooming house. It was a small building on the corner of the block with rooms that overlooked the street. The room was small. It had a bed and a table and one chair. The bathroom was down the hall.

I sat down at the table and wrote a letter home. I couldn't wait to tell my mom and dad what had happened. I wrote a letter telling them that I made the team and that I was going to get paid five hundred dollars a month to play baseball. I also told them in the letter that I would send some money home as soon as I got some.

Being from a little town in the country, I wasn't used to hearing big city noise all night, so I didn't sleep very well. I heard horns blowing, people talking, cars going by, people walking around, and an occasional siren screaming down the street. I really don't think I slept at all that night.

The next morning I mailed my letter home and picked up the piece of paper with the telephone number of Mr. Washington. That telephone number never left my sight. Other than Mr. Crawford, he was the only connection I had to a real person in the big city of Chicago, Illinois. I took the number and went downstairs. I dug in my pocket for a dime and called Mr. Washington from a pay phone. I explained to him who I was and how I appreciated that he took care of my bag for me during my try out. He asked me where I was calling from. I told him I was on the corner of 47 and South Park and he said, "Stand right there, I'll be there shortly."

Within five minutes he was there. He told me to go upstairs and get my bag. "You're coming with me," he said.

I had a good feeling about this man from the start, so I went and got my bag and I went with him to his home. I told him how I had come from Arkansas to try out for the Chicago American Giants and that I was accepted on the team and that we were leaving for Memphis the next morning, on Thursday. Mr. Washington took me to his home. He lived in a three-bedroom apartment on the third floor of the building on 51st Street. It was nicely decorated and I was given my own bedroom for my belongings. That was unbelievable because back in Magnolia I had to share a room with my four brothers and now I would have a whole bedroom to myself.

Mr. Washington began frying up some pork chops. I sat by the kitchen table as he bustled about in the kitchen. I remember the smell of the pork chops frying as I watched him by the stove. We talked about ourselves and got to know each other a little better. When he finished cooking, we ate. Those were the best pork chops I ever had. He served them with rice and gravy. As we enjoyed our dinner, he let me know that I would be staying with him whenever I was in Chicago. I was grateful to know that I now had someone watching out for me in the big city and I thanked him. That night I prayed and thanked the Lord for putting him in my life.

That thank you call was a turning point in my life because Mr. Washington became a father figure to me. Maybe he just felt sorry for me, being as young as I was. Maybe he was just a really nice guy. All I know is that he taught me about life. He taught me about practical things, like how to start a savings account. He fed me when I was in town and gave me a place to sleep and watched over me like I was his own. He was like a father to me and I always say that the Lord put him in my life for a reason. Maybe just to watch over me because I was so young, maybe as a helper for me as I was just starting out, or maybe for me to become a part of his life, which I found out was very empty.

I learned that Mr. Washington had no family. He had a daughter at one time but she died as an infant from a dog bite. She contracted rabies and never recovered. His wife had since moved away and he had not heard a word from her in years. He was pretty much alone until I came along. After awhile he started calling me son and he would introduce me to his friends as his son.

He was an influential force in my life and we remained very close, up until the day he died and I buried him. That was twenty-eight years later.

On Thursday morning, we started off toward Memphis. I was just about out of cash so I didn't have any money when we stopped for sodas on the way. I remember when we stopped at the filling station, a teammate of mine named Clyde McNeal gave me ten dollars. He knew I was broke and he just gave it to me.

"First game pitched by Dennis Biddle"

My first paycheck came the following week on Monday, when we were back in Chicago. It was for one hundred fifty dollars. Mr. Washington helped me start a savings account. I put fifty dollars in my new savings account in the bank. I sent my mother fifty dollars and I paid Clyde McNeal back the ten dollars he had given me. The rest I kept in my pocket. I was rich. I had never had so much money at one time in my whole life. I got used to putting some of my money in my savings account every week and sending some money home to my family on a regular basis.

The next week we had a game in Racine, Wisconsin, against the Philadelphia Stars. I was the starting pitcher and Ted "Double Duty" Radcliffe was my catcher. He was also our team's coach. Double Duty got his nickname from his younger playing days. He used to pitch and catch in the same game. There weren't many players that could do that. He was a great ball player.

He played the game since he was a boy in Mobile, Alabama, and grew up with the legendary Satchel Paige and Bobby Robinson, two other great players from the Negro League. Although he had caught for Satchel since they were kids, Duty's best skill was his pitching according to Bobby Robinson. He said Duty threw a lot of trick balls when he pitched and people had a hard time hitting against him. He was a solid hitter too.

Dennis "Bose" Biddle and Ted "Double Duty" Radcliffe

The Chicago American Giants was the first Negro League team Duty had played for. Andrew "Rube" Foster was his manager. I would learn later that Rube Foster was known as the father of Black baseball because he is the one who founded the Negro Leagues.

I was pitching a game against Gread "Lefty" McKinnis in Racine. He was one of the few pitchers to ever beat Satchel Paige and was known as "the Man Who Beat the Man." As we would pass each other from the mound to the dugout, I could hear him talking to me. He kept telling me, "Kid, you're telegraphing your pitch."

I didn't know what he meant by that so after a few innings I asked Double Duty what Lefty meant by telegraphing your pitch.

Picture of Gread "Lefty" Mckinnis

Double Duty said, "Look, Son, it don't matter what team you're on. If one of the older guys sees you doing something wrong, they'll straighten you out." Double Duty told me that Lefty was trying to help train me and what he meant by telegraphing my pitch was that the batter knew what kind of pitch I was going to throw even before I threw it.

I didn't realize it at the time, but looking back on those older players, they would jump on us about our mistakes, and train us the way it was supposed to be. It was important to them that we played the game the right way because they cared. They wanted us young kids to be the best we could because they felt that we had a chance to get into the majors, and they didn't. So these older players would help train anyone who they felt had potential. It didn't matter if you were on their team or not. They had a common goal to groom us younger players.

It was nice to see the older players help the newcomers. There was no talking back when they tried to help us either. I don't remember any younger player yelling at the older players for giving us tips about our game and helping us learn how to do things right. I just know that I was appreciative of those old men who helped me to play baseball to my fullest potential.

Ted "Double Duty" Radcliffe the oldest living player

I had a good game that day. I got no hits. I struck out, hit a foul ball pop up, and I hit a ball to the pitcher, but I was hot at the mound. I felt really good because I knew I was a decent pitcher, but I didn't know *how* good. They could not hit my sinker (we called them drops). I had a devastating drop, a terrific curve ball, and a sneaky fastball. I struck out thirteen men that day. Big Red hit a home run off me but we still won the game 3-1, and even though I telegraphed my pitch throughout the whole game, I still out-pitched Gread "Lefty" McKinnis. With that win at the age of seventeen, I became known as "the Man Who Beat the Man, Who Beat the Man." I also practiced concealing my pitches from then on.

I won my first five games in the Negro Leagues. I lost the next three. The most humiliating loss for me was when we played against the New York Black Yankees. They gave me my first loss in the Negro League. They scored seven runs off me in the first inning and scored eleven runs by the third. They hit everything I threw at them. Then in the third inning, the coach took me out. I was disappointed because I had heard that they were one of the better teams in the league. I really wanted to beat them but I never got the chance to play against them again. We didn't play them anymore.

The baseball season went by quickly. We played all over the country both in small towns and in Major league stadiums. On our way to a Major league stadium to play a game, our booking agent would book us to play money games with local teams in little towns all the way there. We would play against the local team in that area, and after the booking agent took his ten percent cut off the top of the gate receipts, the remaining money would be split between the two playing teams. The winning team would take sixty percent of the cash and the losing team would take forty percent.

These money games were pretty popular in the smaller cities around the country. Our agent would book us in any little town playing any team and make his ten percent. Then we wouldn't see him for a month. When I look back, the booking agent was probably the one who made the most money during the baseball season.

After the regular season was over, I was invited to play ball overseas. The guys were going to play ball in Caracas, Venezuela, Mexico, and Puerto Rico. I could have made good money but I turned it down because I knew I had to go back to school. Education was very important to me, so I enrolled at an engineering college in Chicago and took up electronics that fall. Looking back on it, though, I wished I had gone with them to play baseball.

Fall turned to winter and I was able to go home for the first time at Christmas. My brother had come home from college and my other brothers and sister was there. Then Mom and Dad came home from work and everyone was happy because we were all together again. They had worried about me being in Chicago but were happy that I was successful. I had kept in touch with my family on a continual basis through letters and phone calls so they always knew I was okay. Nothing much had changed in the little town of Magnolia, Arkansas. My girlfriend had moved on, but that's just part of life.

I left for Chicago shortly after Christmas. It was a long ride back to Chicago but I was ready to get back. I finished out my electronics course that semester and then worked for three months until spring training began.

We traveled by bus wherever we went. As we journeyed across the country, passing through small towns and large cities, I was learning about life and how to survive as a Negro League ballplayer on the road. Being the youngest player on the bus, I was told I had to sit up front with the driver, Wee Willie. Wee Willie was quite a character. He was the only person I had ever met who could eat buffalo fish and make the bones come out the side of his mouth as he chewed. I had never seen anything like it. He told a lot of jokes too, so I enjoyed sitting up front and reading the map for him.

There were a lot of growing pains for me during that period. Not only because I was away from my family for the first time in my life, but because I grew up in a family where I was sheltered a lot and there was love all the time.

Now I was in a very big world with many different attitudes and behaviors I had never seen before. I saw the men I played with cussing each other out on the bus and just about getting into a fight, and then two hours later hugging each other for hitting a home run. I saw a lot of men struggling to get by in the league, too. The reality of life on the road was a big adjustment for me.

It's hard to explain but we were almost like a family. These men were like my fathers because

I was just a teenager and they were in the thirties, forties, and fifties. They called me Kid and they taught me about life. We ate, slept, talked, argued, and played with each other every day.

Very few guys had wives. There were girlfriends in every city for some, but we didn't have time for long relationships. We traveled every day for weeks at a time, traveling south, north, east, and west. It seemed that someone was always trying to hook me up with a niece or a grandkid, but I had no woman on my mind. I was thinking of my professional career.

I think about some of the things that happened to us when we traveled on the bus from city to city and wonder how I ever got along. It was the guys I played ball with who helped me understand what was happening and why, and who encouraged me when I was down.

One of the first things I remember learning about the world was that there was still a great deal of prejudice back then.

I saw a lot of racism and discrimination while we were on the road. Some people we met would treat us badly for no apparent reason. Often times we would have to sleep on the bus because we weren't allowed to sleep in the hotels due to the Jim Crow laws that still governed parts of the South.

Segregation had been a part of my life the whole while I was growing up but I really didn't know any other way. I don't recall experiencing much discrimination at home, probably because we minded our own business and we stayed on our side of town, so I often had difficulty understanding why some white people had such an unfounded distain for me when I was on the road.

I learned that Blacks had been segregated and treated poorly since they were brought to America by ship and sold as slaves sometime around 1619. For years they endured harsh treatment until after the Civil War when they were finally released from captivity. Although Blacks had the new hope of living a modest, if not successful life in the United States, angry white Southerners passed a complex series of laws to keep blacks suppressed, both socially and economically. It started with the Separate Car Act, which led to the famous Plessy vs. Ferguson decision. Separation of the races then spread throughout society like a cancer.

The Separate Car Act was passed in 1890 by the state of Louisiana. It declared that accommodations for Blacks and Whites in the Louisiana railway cars would be "separate but equal."

Two years after the Act was passed, a man named Homére Plessy was jailed for sitting in the White's car on a Louisiana train. Even though Plessy was mostly French (he was only one-eighth Black) and had a pale complexion, he was still considered to be Black under Louisiana law and was therefore mandated to sit in the Colored car. Some stories say he and his friends planned the event to challenge the law and other stories say he just did it on his own. In any case, after refusing to leave the White-only passenger car, the train was stopped and Plessy was arrested and put in jail.

Plessy took his dispute to court and he argued that the Separate Car Act violated the Thirteenth and Fourteenth Amendments of the Constitution, which abolished slavery throughout the United States and made African-Americans citizens.

The judge at the trial was John Howard Ferguson, a lawyer who had once declared the Separate Car Act "unconstitutional on trains that traveled through several states." In Plessy's case, however, Ferguson decided that the State of Louisiana had the right to regulate the railroad companies that operated only within the State of Louisiana, and he found Plessy guilty of refusing to leave the White car.

Although Plessy took his case to the highest court in Louisiana and eventually all the way to the Supreme Court of the United States, the courts stood firm on ruling that separate facilities for Blacks and Whites were constitutional, as long as they were equal. This case set the new standard for the treatment of Blacks.

Segregation quickly spread as the Southern states began to systematically separate the races by passing laws that restricted equal access to public areas including schools, parks, cemeteries, hotels, restaurants, transportation, and even baseball. Local communities posted Whites Only and Colored signs at water fountains, restrooms, waiting rooms, and on access to public buildings such as courthouses, libraries, and theaters.

By 1910, a system of legalized segregation was firmly in place and there were many laws that segregated Blacks from Whites. These laws were referred to as Jim Crow laws.

The term Jim Crow originally came from a minstrel routine called "Jump Jim Crow", which was performed in the early 1800's by Thomas Dartmouth (Daddy) Rice, a white man who painted his face black to imitate a slave. Jim Crow eventually became a word that symbolized stereotypical images of Black's as inferior. It became a derogatory nickname for Blacks, as well as the term used to describe the laws and acts of racial discrimination. These Jim Crow laws continue until the Civil Rights Act, passed in 1964, declared segregation illegal.

When I traveled with the Negro Leagues, it was 1953 so the Jim Crow laws still governed where we could stay. The bus we rode in became our home. It was where we ate when we were not welcome in the area restaurants and where we slept when we were not welcome in public lodging.

When we slept on the bus, everyone scrambled for the back seat because it was long. It was about the only seat on the bus where you could actually lie down somewhat comfortably. I got the back seat only one time. Everyone else had to sleep sitting up because there wasn't any room to lie down. We would put all the equipment on the floor and sleep sitting up in the seats. I didn't mind because most of the time we would stay up and tell jokes or talk about life until the wee hours of the morning anyway.

Not having a place to stay also meant that we couldn't take a shower. There were times when we couldn't shower for two or three days. Some of the older player knew where there were water holes off the highway, though, so we would often stop at a watering hole to wash our clothes. Showers, unfortunately, were not so easily found.

We weren't always welcome to eat in the area restaurants either. Several days might go by before we could find a place to serve us, so we usually ate our meals on the bus. When we would stop for gas we would buy up all the bologna and light bread we could find to make bologna sandwiches on the bus. Mr. Brewer always said that bologna was a delicacy because at the time, it was the best food we could get!

I usually ate a sandwich, drank a Nehigh soda and had a little something for dessert. I always got a Stage Plank cookie, a ginger cookie with pink icing for dessert, if I could. Those were my favorites.

Because we had to make sandwiches and eat in the bus most of the time, we sure got sick of the sandwiches. If we ever stopped for gas and there were a little store near by, we would go and buy up all the crackers and sardines they had. Sardines and crackers was a delicacy to us. My auntie ate sardines all the time when I was a child, and I didn't like the smell of them so I never ate them. But I was so hungry one day I finally ate some and found that I liked them. I laughed at myself because I could have been eating these for years but I would never try them. And let me tell you, you never witnessed any smell like a bus full of baseball players who hadn't showered in two days, eating sardines and crackers!

Eating and sleeping on the bus was a novelty for me and it was kind of fun, but for the older guys it wasn't fun. You could see it on their face that it wasn't fun for them. It was arduous and disgraceful for a professional ballplayer but it was an unfortunate reality for us.

There were also many places where we weren't even allowed to use the public restroom.

The road trips were long, but pleasant enough. We would chat for hours while we drove across the country. Sometimes it was so hot on the bus we would be dripping by the time we finally got off when we stopped for gas and something to drink.

One time, in the southern heat of Kentucky, we drove up to a filling station to get gas and saw that they had a well in the back. We asked the lady if we could get a drink of water and she politely showed us to the well. There was a gourd hanging off the side of the well so we drew the water up and we all drank from the gourd.

We thanked her and got back on the bus. As the bus went up a little hill with a turn, I could see back to the filling station where we had just been. I watched with curiosity as the lady who had given us permission to drink from her well walked around to the back of the building. She picked up the gourd we had used to drink and began to smash it into pieces on the side of the well. I naively thought maybe she did that whenever any strangers drank from the well, but I could tell it was more than that when I saw James "Cool Papa" Bell just shake his head in disgust and look away.

There were some places we looked forward to visiting where we knew we wouldn't have to sleep or eat on the bus. Birmingham was one place where we knew we could get a bed. There were always fans at the ball park who would rent room and board to the players after the game. I would always be sure to find someone to rent from who could cook. The next day we would talk about where we stayed and how our evening was.

Memphis was another place where we knew we could get a hotel bed. When we went to Memphis the players would head to Beal Street where they had a lot of nightclubs. Cool Papa Bell would always make us wear a tie and a suit whenever we went out. He would say, "You're professionals and you're gonna act like it."

I liked that about him. He felt that acting in a professional manner was important no matter where you played or who you played for. Everybody in town especially the women, knew who the ball players were when they came out on the town. I snuck into a couple of the clubs, but most of the time they would catch me and throw me out.

When I couldn't get in, I would go to the movies or go back to the hotel and talk to some of the older guys that didn't go out. Sometimes I would get pointers for the next game I was to pitch. We had a few pitchers so we were rotated. I usually pitched, and then for the next few days in a row I would play center, shortstop, first, or second base. Whenever I pitched, I would tell the

who wanted to watch and collected two hundred forty dollars. That wasn't a whole lot of money but we won the game and split it among the guys.

Plrasr refere to Picture #12-13

I, _Ted 'Double Duty' Radcliffe_, certify that _Dennis 'Bose' Biddle_ was a team mate of mine in 1953 with the Chicago American Giants. I was the catcher in his first professional game against the Memphis Red Sox, at Martin Stadium in Memphis, Tennessee.

Ted 'Double Duty' Radcliffe

Notary Public ---   (Seal)

NOTARY PUBLIC
MONICA A. HECK
STATE OF WISCONSIN

The next day the bus had a flat tire. We were on our way to Kansas City. Wee Willie made all of us get off the bus and take all of our equipment off. All sixteen of us got out and stood by the side of the road with our equipment, watching as Wee Willie jacked up the bus. Suddenly the bus fell. The teeth on the jack were stripped. We were surprised, but relieved that Wee Willie wasn't hurt. We all got together and lifted the bus while Wee Willie put on the spare tire. Sweaty and exhausted, we slowly let the bus down, only to realize that the spare tire was flat too! After a good laugh and some exhausted sighs, we picked the bus back up again so Wee Willie could get the spare tire back off.

Meanwhile, a car stopped and the person in the car drove two of the guys into town to fix the tire. We sat at the side of the road and after a few hours they returned, and once again we lifted the bus while Wee Willie put on the tire. We finally reloaded our equipment and went on our way to Kansas City.

As we traveled the country playing ball and surviving, I grew very fond of these men that I traveled with. They taught me a lot in two years. They were my mentors. They were my fathers and they prepared me for what I would face in the future just as they had Jackie Robinson, Hank Aaron, Ernie Banks, and many, many more young players in the Negro League.

They were my teachers too, and the stories they told me were history. We didn't have stats or history books about those who played before us, just the stories from those who played with and against them. Our history was passed down verbally from one generation to the next and that's how I learned about the Negro League and the legendary athletes who played before me.

I think it is important to note that baseball was an integrated sport until the late 1800's. Shortly after the Civil War, Blacks played with Whites on competitive leagues. Later, baseball went professional and the many Jim Crow laws were passed. Baseball hired a commissioner named Kenesaw Landis. When he came into power, everything changed. Landis was racially prejudiced and used the "separate but equal" philosophy to initiate an era of nearly fifty years of segregated baseball.

Landis arranged for the owners of the baseball teams meet to set up some common rules for the game, including who would be on their respective teams and how they would recruit new players. During one of these meetings, they secretly agreed to oust Blacks from the league. The owners all agreed that no one would hire a Black man to play on their team ever again. This agreement was not something that was written down, but was a gentlemen's agreement. Blacks already playing for a team would not have their contracts renewed and the majority of owners agreed that no one would hire a Black to play on their baseball team in the future. Although some owners felt that was unfair and tried unsuccessfully to keep Blacks playing, the majority ruled and thus began the color barrier in Major league baseball.

Blacks, however, did not let that stop them from playing the game. They formed their own teams and barnstormed around the country playing with and against each other until 1920 when a man named Andrew "Rube" Foster organized the first all-Black baseball league.

Rube Foster had been a great pitcher in his playing days, but he was a great businessman too. He wanted his league to compare to the majors and he was the reason Black baseball became both respectable and financially successful.

The league he organized was called the Negro League and in the twenties and thirties it flourished along side Major League baseball, grooming some of the best baseball players in history.

American Giants Base Ball Club

ANDREW (RUBE) FOSTER, CLUB MANAGER

THE GREATEST AGGREGATION OF COLORED
BASE BALL PLAYERS IN THE WORLD

Park Located at 39th St. and Wentworth Ave.

(WHITE SOX OLD GROUNDS)

· FINEST SEMI-PRO. PARK IN THE U. S.

OWNED AND OPERATED BY

JOHN M. SCHORLING, OFFICE, 403 WEST 79TH STREET

To many people, Black baseball was more entertaining than White baseball and it drew a lot of fans, both Black and White, throughout the years. Blacks didn't play the game quite the same as White players. Some Black teams entertained their fans with shadow ball, a mimed version of baseball, and with many tricks they incorporated into the game to make it more interesting, including the bunt. These variations made Black baseball a more daring and more interesting game to watch than major league games.

A legendary pitcher, Satchel Paige, was so confident that he would sometimes throw his first pitch to the first batter with no one in the outfield to back him up. These activities made the Negro League baseball games fun and exciting to watch. At times, a whole town would shut down to go watch Satchel Paige pitch a game at the local field.

Negro League ball players had three options if they wanted to make money. They would play in their regular league games against other Negro League teams, they could go barnstorming across the country, playing in small towns against local teams and they could play in the occasional games that were set up in different cities across the country where Blacks from the Negro League would play against Whites from the major league.

These Black-against-White games drew big crowds. Too often though, the Negro League team would beat their Major league competitors. Eventually Landis, the commissioner of Major League Baseball, wanted to forbid his major league players from playing against the Negro Leaguers because they were beaten too many times and it made the White teams look bad.

He told the major league ball club owners not to play against the Blacks because the Blacks had everything to gain and the Whites had everything to lose. If the major league players won, it was no big deal because they were supposedly better than Black ball players anyway, but if they lost, which they often did, not only did they look bad being beaten by Blacks, but it might cause concern in Major League baseball. After all, if these Blacks were good enough to beat the major league teams, then why weren't they allowed to play in the majors? It would seem unreasonable.

Unfortunately, Negro League ball players didn't get paid like Major League ball players either. Sadly, they got paid quite a bit less, even though the play was just as competitive as the major leagues.

Negro League ball players did play the game of baseball a little differently than Whites (with a few added twists, many of which were eventually adopted by the majors), but this was no reason for the pay discrepancy.

Not only was their pay far less than that of a Major Leaguer, Negro League ball players were also not afforded insurance, or medical care if they got injured during the game. A lot of the players had to play injured or they didn't get paid, so you would see guys out there on the field with broken fingers, sprained ankles, or pulled hamstrings, playing just to make their paycheck. Many of the players who had to play with injuries are still suffering today due to the repercussions of untreated injuries from years ago.

Unlike the Major League ball players, Negro League ball players were only paid when they actually played a ball game. Unlike their major league counterparts, there were few rests in between games, if they could help it. So Negro League ballplayers usually played in as many games as they could. Sometimes they would play as many as three or four games in a day, in two different cities.

Their booking agent would set up these games all across the country each season. Negro League ball players would play in these money games in between their regularly scheduled games.

Because Negro League players' contracts were not binding at the time, Negro League ball players could play for anyone they wanted. So the ball players would travel around the country by bus during the hot, sticky summer then many would go south of the border during winter months to continue playing – and getting paid – for different baseball teams.

They also tended to play for any team that would offer them more money to play. The older players told me that's how Leroy Paige got his nickname Satchel. Every time another team would pay him more money than the team he was on, he would grab his bag and switch teams to make more money. He got paid very well for it too.

Many great ballplayers played in the Negro Leagues but since statistics were not kept, most of their record-breaking feats went unnoticed by the major leagues and by society in general. We didn't need stats. We knew who was good. Players like Satchel Paige. Before my time, he was one of the most noted pitchers in the Negro Leagues. He was tall and thin and had a great arm. Sometimes he would wind up for a pitch and sometimes he wouldn't. I was told he could consistently pitch a baseball over a piece of cloth. He was also a great showman. He named his fast balls. As a matter of fact, his fast balls were thrown so hard that helmets were first worn in the game to protect batters from his pitching. He also had developed what he called a hesitation pitch, where he paused for just a second before letting the ball go. That pause threw off batters' timing so badly that they couldn't hit the ball.

Leroy Paige finally went to the major leagues in 1948, when he was in his mid-forties. He was the oldest rookie to ever play in the major leagues. He lost money by going to the major leagues, but he wanted the credibility so that's why he went.

Josh Gibson was another great ball player. He was never given a chance in the majors. He was noted as being the Black Babe Ruth. He once hit a ball completely out of Yankee Stadium. No one had ever done that before, or since. He had over eighty homeruns in one season, but that did not matter to the major leagues. He still went unrecognized. Josh died of a stroke two months before Jackie Robinson entered the major leagues.

In 2003, Barry Bonds, Jr., current home run record in baseball, finally gave Josh Gibson the rightful public recognition he deserved in a news article in the *Milwaukee Journal Sentinel*. It was heartwarming to see that someone finally stood up for the truth. He stated, "If Josh Gibson hit eighty-four home runs in one season, then he is the home run record holder. It's not me, statistically. It belongs to Josh Gibson." (*Milwaukee Journal Sentinel*, July 15, 2003, p. 3C).

Cool Papa Bell was another awesome player in the Negro Leagues. Cool Papa Bell was a traveling mentor when I came into the Negro Leagues. He was a mentor to the younger players on my team and to other players on other teams in the League. He mentored me, but also any young person who had enough talent to make it to the majors. Personally, I think he was a type of training scout for the majors but he never said he was, and I have no proof. I only know he spent a lot of time working with me when he was with us. Maybe he took a special interest in me because of my speed although I was no where as fast as him. We became good friends and it was through him that I learned so much about the Negro League. Through the years we stayed in touch and remained friends.

James "Cool Papa" Bell was one of the fastest ball players to ever run the bases. He could run from first to third base on a bunt! He was so fast that others joked about him being able to shut off the light and be in bed before it got dark in the room.

It is documented that one time during an inter-racial all-star exhibition game on the West Coast, Satchel Paige hit a bunt with Cool Papa Bell on first base. As the catcher of the Indians got ready to throw to first base, Cool Papa Bell darted past him to score.

He was a living legend. I didn't know that at the time. As far as I knew, he was just one of the trainers. He never talked much about himself. I just knew he could run real fast. I was fast too, but no one could run the bases like Cool Papa. Later I learned he was the fastest man ever to play the game.

Although he was certainly good enough to go to the majors, he never went and he rarely talked about it. The only thing he told me was that when Branch Rickie approached him about it, he cursed him out. He said he asked Rickie, "Why didn't you ask me twenty years ago?"

Before Mr. Bell died, he said something that is quoted often and may go down in the history books as a blemish on America's conscience. He said, "So many people say I was born too early. But that's not true. They opened the doors too late."

Throughout my travels in the Negro League, I also learned about some of the remarkable players I played with and against.

Besides our playing coach, Ted "Double Duty" Radcliffe, we had Clyde McNeal and Art Pennington on our team. Clyde McNeil was one of the greatest shortstops I have ever seen play and Art "Superman" Pennington was our first baseman. He was a great hitter. Cool Papa Bell said that Superman was one of the players who should have been in the major leagues.

Carl Long was another great player. I played against him. He was a powerful hitter with the Birmingham Black Barons during the time when I played with the Chicago American Giants. One day at a game at Comiskey Park, he hit a line drive off me that hit the left field wall for a double. To this day he still brags about the time he hit this hanging curveball off the left field wall of old Comiskey Park, against me, in the seventh inning. The funny part is that he always forgets to mention that I struck him out his first two times up!

The history books tell some interesting things about the Negro Leagues, but just like Christopher Columbus didn't really discover America (it had been inhabited for years), the history books left out a great deal when it comes to the real truth about the Negro Baseball Leagues.

I learned a lot riding on that bus. As I said before, we passed our history down by word-of-mouth. There was no need to write it down. Everyone knew the truth. While on the bus and in the dusty makeshift dugouts of the small baseball fields where we played, this good friend of mine, who had been in the leagues since before the Depression in the thirties, told me some little-known facts about the Negro League and what was actually happening to them as we spoke.

"You see," he said during a long, hot and muggy summer afternoon, "in the beginning he taught me that most of the Negro League owners were Black. He said times were good and Black baseball was a successful business. That was, until the Depression hit. Then the Negro Leagues that Rube Foster had started began to fold because of the bad economic times.

After the Depression; after Rube Foster was gone and most of the teams had folded, White businessmen saw what a money maker Black baseball was and how the Black teams drew in scores of fans, sometimes more fans than the White teams. They certainly didn't want to see all that money go to waste, so with greed in their hearts and a lie on their lips, they brought back some of the Negro League teams that had folded.

But at that time Black businessmen didn't really own the teams. They were used to front, as the owners of the teams, but Whites were really the ones who owned most of the teams. My friend told me that if I went to a lot of the older players who are living today and asked them who owned their team they would give me a name, but it wasn't the name of the real owner, because the real owners are White and not a lot of people know that. There were some Black owners, he said, but most of the owners after the Depression were White.

Sixteen teams made up the new post-Depression Negro League. Four of those teams dropped out over the years, leaving twelve teams that comprised the Negro Leagues. This time however, most of the Negro League team owners were White. And that was the downfall of the Negro Baseball League, he told me. Even in 1953 he knew we were going to start to die out as a league.

My friend told me that the White team owners would set up money making ventures for their Black teams. Sometimes they would get major league teams to play their Black teams and sometimes they were able to negotiate with the major league to use their ball parks for their Black teams. Anyone who knows about the history of the Black man in the United States knows that it would be difficult at best, for a Black owner to negotiate a place in a major league park back then, so it made sense to me that Whites must have really owned most of the Negro League teams.

As a result, the Negro League teams began to be able to play in the major league parks. These Negro League games would sometimes draw more fans than the Major league games and it was a great boost for the credibility of the Negro teams.

It was about this time when Kenesaw Landis, of Major League Baseball died, and the new commissioner, "Happy" Chandler took over. According to the history books, Chandler is said to have wanted baseball integrated to reverse the unfair, unspoken order of Kenesaw Landis. Chandler could never admit there was an official color line because according to the majors, that order never existed. In 1944, rumors were already surfacing that Major league scouts might begin to recruit Blacks to the Major league.

But truth be known, there was a lot more at stake for Happy Chandler than just repealing an unfair, racial injustice. My friend told me that the Major league players were consistently losing to their Negro League counterparts and this was a serious concern for Happy Chandler when he came aboard as Commissioner of baseball. It was also embarrassing, so Happy Chandler needed to find a way out for the major leagues.

Having the Negro League teams playing in the Major league parks and drawing more fans than his all-White Major league teams was a big economical concern too, so Happy Chandler called a meeting of the owners and explained why they had to do something about this.

The ugly truth of the matter was that the major leagues wouldn't let Blacks play with them but they were letting them use their Major league parks to play their Negro League ball games and the Black teams were drawing more fans than the Major league teams. Besides that, whenever the Major league teams played against the Negro League teams, the White teams seemed to lose! That was bad for business. The bigger problem, of course, was that there was never a public pronouncement that Blacks were ever banned from Major league baseball. Remember, it was just a gentleman's agreement. They could not just "open the door" because in theory, it had never been closed!

I was told that the major league owners decided that the best thing to do was to raise the rent for the Negro League owners to rent a major league ballpark. But the Negro Leagues continued to draw more and more fans, and remained successful.

There was a consensus that the only way to save the integrity, and the business, of the major leagues was to allow Blacks to play with them. Most of the owners were reluctant to take a chance on doing this, except for Branch Rickie. But it isn't the entire story.

It was no secret that sooner or later Blacks would be allowed to play in the major leagues one day. Happy Chandler even stated that he would not oppose Negroes playing in the major leagues. There was also a lot of pressure from a lot of different groups to allow Blacks to play in the majors. After all, Blacks had fought and died in World War II along side of Whites for the sake of their country, why couldn't they play baseball together? Some of the owners didn't like the barrier but they didn't say much about it. Others still did not want to integrate baseball.

My friend told me that Branch Rickey, general manager of the Brooklyn Dodgers, was a clever businessman and he knew that sooner or later, Negroes would be playing in the major leagues. He told me that Branch Rickey wanted Blacks to play in the majors and had permission to scout for Black players if he chose. But he knew that if the door were open completely, there would be too many Blacks coming in at once and he knew that society wasn't ready to allow that to happen. Remember, segregation was still legal, alive, and well.

About ten years before my time in the Negro League, Branch Rickey had started an all-Black baseball team called the Brown Dodgers. Although they folded soon after they got started, they were around long enough for Branch Rickey to see some great Black athletes in the Negro League.

Being a sound businessman, Branch Rickey thought that because society would never allow Blacks to just flood the majors, it would be a great idea to use this plethora of great young Black ball players as a minor league system for the majors. That way, major league teams could bring in a few of the best Black ball players one at a time.

He also knew that the first one who crossed over would have to be someone who understood that though they were opening the door ever so slightly, they couldn't open it all the way just yet.

He knew that this person would either make it or break it for future Blacks to enter the majors, so this person would have to be able to take the verbal and possible physical abuse of being the first and only Black man on a team of white players. Rickey wasn't looking for the best ball player; he was looking for someone with the inner strength and the right attitude to do what had to be done.

So, before anyone even thought to do it, Branch Rickey interviewed hundreds of Negro League ball players, including my good friend who told me these things, but none of them proved to be the type of person Rickey needed to cross the color line.

He needed to find someone who could withstand the suffering he would have to go through to break the fifty-seven-year color barrier that started with the non-renewal of Fleetwood Walker's contract back in the late 1800's. He needed a strong person who wouldn't fight back with his fists, but with his skill at the game.

Then Jackie Robinson came along. After interviewing him, Rickey knew that Jackie would be able to handle the disparagement and use his batting skills, his fielding skills, and running ability to combat the ridicule he would receive in the major league. Jackie wasn't the best player of the Negro Leagues, my friend told me, but Jackie was solid and he had class, and more importantly, he understood what Branch Rickey was trying to do.

Because Jackie's contract with the Negro League was not binding, and Jackie could play wherever he chose, Rickey took him from the Negro Leagues and signed him with the Brooklyn Dodgers organization in Montreal. At first, it seemed to be a blessing that Jackie broke the color barrier but it was really a deathblow to the Negro Leagues. My friend told me that Branch Rickey knew that as soon as the first Black player crossed into the major leagues, it would break up the dynasty of the Negro Leagues. My friend described it as the end of an era, and the beginning of the demise of the Negro Leagues.

Soon after Jackie signed, the Cleveland Indians organization signed Larry Dobe. His contract with the Negro League was not binding, so he left to play with the majors too, and the Negro League got nothing in return for either of their players.

This upset the Negro League owners and they quickly came up with a resolution. They would now make all new Negro League ball players sign long binding contracts so that if the majors wanted them, they would have to purchase their contracts from the Negro League team he was on. That would at least give them something for their loss.

That meant that the major leagues were forced to purchase players' contracts from the Negro Leagues if they wanted them. That also meant that Negro Leaguers couldn't jump from team to team anymore.

Although that was the case, there were still a lot of young players being signed to play for the Negro League. Willie Mays ((Birmingham Black Barons, 1950), Hank Aaron (Indianapolis Clowns, 1952), and Ernie Banks (Kansas City Monarchs, 1953) were just a few.

Other Negro League ball players that had their binding contracts bought out by the majors before me were Roy Campanella, Don Newcomb, Monte Irvin, and Joe Black. There were more signed each and every year after Jackie Robinson. My friend often called those being signed by the major leagues their token Black players because there were very few being signed. At the time I had joined the Negro League in 1953, there were twenty black players signed by only seven major league teams. They all left the Negro Leagues for the majors when their contract was bought out from the Negro League team they were on.

My friend explained to me that the contract I signed was a binding contract too, and if the major leagues wanted me they would have to buy out my contract from the Chicago American Giants.

He said that some of the money the Negro League was getting for the players that were going to major league was to pay the older players like him, and that is how the Negro League was going to stay alive in the future. We didn't know it at the time but we were dying a long, slow death due to the greed of the Negro League owners.

My friend said that Branch Rickie knew taking Jackie Robinson would change things for both the major leagues and the Negro Leagues and he originally planned to use the Negro Leagues as a minor league system for the majors. He said he would have preferred that for three reasons. He said it would have given us a better chance to get into the majors, and it would have made the transition into the majors an easier one for us. He also said it would have given our League more credibility in the baseball world. Looking back, it also would have given the Negro League ball players still living today some credibility, too.

My friend went on to tell me that when Branch Rickie got ready to implement his plan, the White owners of the Negro Leagues refused to cooperate because they figured they could get more money by selling our contracts to the major leagues. In other words, Branch Rickie's long-range plan to use the Negro League as a minor league system backfired on him because most of the owners refused his offer to use them as a minor league system. My guess is that they probably figured that the Negro League's days were numbered no matter what happened, so they might as well make a few bucks off the major leagues while they could.

So for the next several years, the major league continued to use us as their source to find players by buying out our contracts, but that would only last so long.

It was sad that the White owners of the Negro League gave no concern to what their refusal to cooperate would do to the Negro League, or to us, in the future. My friend told me that the owners didn't care if we died out or not, as long as they got their money.

Because the owners continued to refuse to cooperate, the majors then started recruiting Black players from the same sources as the Negro League. So, not only did the major leagues buy out most of the young star players of the Negro League, they also began to go to the playgrounds, high schools, and colleges to recruit new Black players, just like the Negro Leagues had done for years. They had tapped the Negro League of its younger star players, and now they were impeding other young Black players from joining the Negro League by taking them straight into the majors.

That's why players who otherwise would have been in the Negro League first went right to the major leagues. The majors went and recruited the Black ball players themselves. Guys like Reggie Jackson, Frank Robinson, Barry Bonds, Sr. and many other black players never had to go through the Negro Baseball League because it was at the time when the major leagues were getting players from all sources.

When Jackie Robinson signed with the major leagues, most of the focus moved from watching the Negro League ball games to watching him and other Blacks trickle in to the majors.

After awhile, no one seemed to notice the Negro Leagues or the old men who were left behind. Those who played for the Negro League and then went on to the majors never looked back, and those who were taken from other sources never had the opportunity to play for the Negro Leagues before joining the majors so they didn't know what was really happening.

Once the real owners felt they couldn't make any more money selling our contracts to the majors, they split, and by 1958 or so, there were only a few black owners left struggling to hold the League together by owning two or three teams. Over the next few years, the teams that were left in the Negro League could not compete for top Black players any more and they simply faded away. Mr. Brewer said so often that there is no legal document in the country that dictated the end of the Negro League – it just died.

Although Jackie Robinson broke the color barrier seven years prior to my joining the Negro Leagues, the racial barrier was alive and well and would not be truly broken for years to come. It took almost twelve years for every major league team to have at least one minority on their roster. It wasn't until 1959, when the Boston Red Sox signed Pumpsie Green to their ball club, that every major league team had at least one Black man on their roster. Pumpsie Green was the last ball player from the Negro Leagues to be signed into the majors.

I played in the Negro League for two years. I felt that the Negro League was still going strong at that time. At the end of the 1954 baseball season, I received a letter from the owner of our team, Frank Crawford, saying that the Chicago Cubs had purchased my contract from the Chicago American Giants. I was very satisfied with the news that I was finally going to get my shot at the majors. I knew I was good enough; I was just waiting for someone to see me play and offer me the opportunity. The letter said that the Cubs would be sending me a plane ticket to join them for their spring training so I spent the off-season preparing myself to join the major leagues.

In the spring of 1955, I boarded a plane from Chicago to Arizona. I was satisfied and content to know that I had finally been offered a try out as a non-roster player for the Chicago Cubs. I reported to spring training with confidence and anticipation.

On the first day of practice, during a running exercise, I slid into third base and immediately felt a shooting pain in my leg. As I lay on the field looking up at the sun, many thoughts ran through my mind. I was disgusted. I knew my leg was broken but I was hoping this wouldn't be the end of my baseball career.

The team doctor came over and gave me a shot to ease the pain and I was taken to the hospital. They told me my ankle was broken in two places. They put a cast on it and they told me to come in once a week for therapy.

I worked very hard to get myself back to normal so I could play again. After six long, frustrating months, I felt I was able to pitch and run as well as I ever could. I met with the team doctor and he examined me. Then he told me the news I didn't want to hear. He told me he was sorry, but I would not be able to pitch in the major leagues. My heart sank deep down into the pit of my stomach. That news was more devastating to me than when I wasn't drafted into the majors back in high school.

Although I was paid until my contract ended, it was no consolation to me. I was beside myself with agony that I couldn't play professional ball anymore. I felt like my life was over. I had worked so hard to get where I was in baseball. I loved baseball and my life-long goal was to play in the major league and now I couldn't do that.

After some serious soul-searching, I realized that I had my chance, but the Lord didn't intend for me to play baseball for a living. He intended for me to do something else, so I decided once again to go back to school.

I moved to Milwaukee in 1958 and I opened a TV radio repair shop while I went back to school. I ran my shop for seven years. It was a successful business.

In school, I had taken up drafting. I wanted to know how to read blueprint but I gave that up because my drawing skills weren't that great. Then I enrolled in a welding class and began working for a company as a welder. One day I decided I didn't want to do that any more, so I started working for Job Service as a job counselor. That is when I decided to get a college degree in social work. I closed up my television repair shop and seriously took to the books.

I went to the University of Wisconsin—Milwaukee while I continued to work for the state, and got my degree in social work. I worked in Job Service thirteen years and then I went to work at the Ethan Allen School for boys. I worked there for eleven years as a social worker, and then retired.

In between, I had gotten married and had nine wonderful children, two of whom were adopted.

"It's unreal to me what you read when you look at books having to do with the Negro Leagues. Sometimes they tell it like it was but most of the time it is just fiction. Entertainment. I want the true history to come out." I was in the Negro Leagues long enough to learn about what had happened and what was happening, and now I intend to pass that on to future generations.

—Dennis Biddle

CHAPTER TWO

It was October 1995. I received a letter inviting me to a reunion. The Negro Leagues Baseball Museum in Kansas City, Missouri, invited all the living players from the Negro Baseball Leagues together to celebrate the 75th Anniversary of Negro League Baseball. There would be food and fun, a big banquet, an autograph-signing session, and a group picture taken on the infield of Satchel Paige Memorial Stadium. The many sponsors of the museum paid for our flight, transportation, hotel room, and all of our meals. All we had to do was show up, have our picture taken, and sign a few autographs. I was excited. It sounded like it would be a lot of fun. But more than that, it would be the first time in fifty years that former teammates from the Negro Leagues would see each other again.

Two weeks prior to this event, a sports talk show host in Milwaukee, Wisconsin, called to see if he could get a live interview with me on the telephone while I was in Kansas City for the reunion. He said this was going to be a great human-interest story. I agreed to the interview and told him that I would call him from the hotel once I had arrived.

Thursday, October 26, 1995

I boarded the plane in Milwaukee and flew to Kansas City. Several other players were on the same plane, although I didn't know it at the time. When we got off the plane in Kansas City, there was a man standing with a sign that read, "Negro Leagues." Seeing that sign sent a flood of memories to my mind. Suddenly, I realized I was about to be reintroduced to a life that was so important to me when I was growing up. It was so long ago. I thought I would never see the day when I would reunite with my past and with the rich history of which I was a part. I was suddenly anxious to get to where all the players were.

Eventually, about seven men and their spouses walked up to the man with the sign and we all headed for the door. I didn't recognize any of them. Outside the airport there were several limos waiting to escort us to the hotel. As the limo drove us to the hotel, there was an inexplicable silence in the car. Anticipation filled the air. I longed to see the people I had played with so many years ago, but didn't know what to expect.

As I entered the lobby of the hotel, I was speechless. There were droves of people there. Most of the players who had arrived were assembled in the lobby of the hotel. Television crews and newspaper reporters from all over the world were swarming around them, vying for interviews. There was energy in the air. I was overwhelmed, but at the same time felt content and very much at home.

I went to check in at the sign-in table set up for the players. There I was given a badge to wear. They gave me a packet containing my itinerary and other pertinent information for the weekend including my room number, tickets for the banquet and dinner, information on the autograph session, the picture we were to take, the BBQ, and every other event for which we were expected to be present. The itinerary read that there would be five buses, one for wheelchairs, available to transfer us from place to place that weekend. A number was on my itinerary to let me know which bus I should ride. They also asked that we all tour the Negro Leagues Baseball Museum while we were here to celebrate our place in history.

After I gathered my things I went to the front desk, got my room key, and took my luggage to the room. It was around 3:00 pm. After quickly unpacking, I rushed back down to the lobby where television crews and reporters were still bustling about. The energy in the room was exhilarating. Men were laughing and talking and greeting each other. I didn't recognize many people but I kept hearing, "There's the Kid," and I knew I was among friends.

I started talking to several players, asking them to volunteer to be interviewed on the radio, via telephone, in Milwaukee. Several players agreed. One of them was one of the oldest living players at that time, Ted "Double Duty" Radcliffe. (He turned 101 years old on June 6, 2003.) He caught for the legendary Satchel Paige of the Kansas City Monarchs. He also caught the first game I ever pitched for the Chicago American Giants. "Boy, he could bring it," he said, referring to how hard I used to throw. He showed us his hands and kept calling me, "Kid".

We visited until 6:00 pm, then I gathered some of the guys for the telephone interview with the radio station in Milwaukee. I called the station but it was too loud for them to hear us so we were unable to finish the interview. Somewhat disappointed, I hung up the telephone and continued to mingle. After hours flew by, I finally went upstairs to get some sleep.

I was up several times during the night. I was just too excited to settle down. I finally went back down to the lobby to see if anyone was still there. I arrived to the same scene as before, former baseball legends being interviewed by reporters, being filmed and photographed, hugging and reminiscing about their past, and celebrating their lives. I sat down and joined in the conversations, talking with old friends until after 1:00 am. Then, exhausted, I went to my room and finally slept.

Friday, October 27, 1995

At 8:00 am I boarded a bus with about forty other players to go to the autograph session in downtown Kansas City. We were each paid for our time to sign autographs for two hours. When we arrived at the site, I saw what must have been thousands of people lined up for blocks waiting to get into the building just to get our autographs. As I sat in my designated seat at a table, I again felt so proud to be a part of the history that was unfolding.

Outside, people purchased a ticket for each autograph they wanted. As they came into the building, each person received a 75th anniversary souvenir card. We signed their card along with anything else they had brought for an autograph. I must have signed five hundred autographs in those two hours.

When the next busload of players came, we left and went back to the hotel. We had a bite to eat, relaxed for a short time, and then a group of us decided to go see the Negro Leagues Baseball Museum.

The museum is a wonderful place. It was very enjoyable to see some of our past being displayed. After all these years we finally had a concrete place in history. I felt comfort knowing there was finally a site that represented the contributions we made to the history of baseball.

After our tour we were each asked to autograph a huge baseball bat for the museum to display once the reunion was over. We obliged and then left to go back to the hotel to get ready for our 6:00 dinner.

A bus took us to a famous barbeque place for dinner and a reception where the mayor of Kansas City gave us a proclamation. During the course of the evening I was introduced to him and several other elected representatives of the city. After dinner, a famous singer entertained us while we danced and reminisced until it was time to go back to the hotel.

We congregated in the lobby once again when we returned. The television cameras carried on twenty-four hours a day during our entire stay. I can't remember ever seeing such a happy group of men in my life. They hadn't seen each other in fifty years and they were just joyful to be together one more time. I was at ease mingling, resting in my room for short periods of time, and then mingling some more while the newspaper reporters, magazine reporters, and television reporters continued interviewing us.

I met many players and we shared our unique stories about the Negro Baseball Leagues with each other. I signed and received autographs from these legends and it was exceptionally satisfying. After many stories and pictures and autographs, I finally went to bed. It was 5:00 am.

Saturday, October 28, 1995

I woke up and men who had not gone to sleep were still in the hotel lobby with the never-ending barrage of television crews and interviews continually taking place. I felt like a celebrity because people from all over the world were competing for our attention. It was surreal. We ate and then went to get ready for our photograph session.

Five buses left in a caravan for Satchel Paige Stadium at 1:00 pm. When we reached the stadium, the buses ceremoniously circled the infield while people in the stands cheered and took pictures. It was then that I realized that these five buses were carrying some of the greatest baseball players of all time. There were over two hundred of us. Two hundred living baseball players left from a momentous time long ago. It was a historic day in the lives of these people from the Negro Baseball Leagues. It was a precious day. A short five years after this event, nearly one hundred of us had passed away and the number of these living legends continues to decrease today. Soon there will be no one left to share our stories.

The buses came to a stop, and as I stepped off the bus the magnitude of this experience once again overwhelmed me. We had come from all over the country just to be here together today, some clutching canes, and others pushed in wheelchairs. I could hardly believe I was here. I have so many fond memories of the people I met and of the places I saw when I played for the Negro Leagues. It was an extraordinary experience for me. And now, forty years later I took the field once again with some of the greatest ballplayers in the history of baseball.

Cameras flashed from all directions as we assembled around the infield. Tears welled in my eyes as I looked around me. We were each given a number to put on our jacket, which identified who we were, and a baseball to autograph for a picture we would take later. The television camera crews in the stands took photographs while the fans watched and recorded this once-in-a-lifetime event. The press and the public kept snapping pictures and the television cameras kept filming.

For one photo, we all threw the baseball we signed into the air at the count of three. In another, we all faced home plate. And after a long period of picture-taking, we were asked to leave our ball in the place where we were standing on the field and get back on the buses to go to the banquet. Our wives had already been escorted to the banquet by bus and were waiting for us. For some reason this seemed very symbolic to me. To me it represented teammates and friends going their separate ways and our past being left behind.

Picture from 1995 Negro League 75 year reunion

We met up with our spouses and started the celebration. The banquet was at a downtown hotel. It was unique and enjoyable. We ate and then Buck O'Neil spoke. Buck O'Neil was a former Negro Leagues baseball player and manager of the Kansas City Monarchs. He was one of the better-known players there. He had gotten a job as the chairman for the museum in Kansas City and many of us regarded him as a leader for us, as a group. An announcement was then made that there would be a meeting in the morning in the hotel conference room before we headed home. No one knew what it would be about, but this was the meeting that changed the course of my life forever.

After the banquet we all went back to the hotel. By this time it was well after midnight. Within an hour, the television crews were back to the hotel too. The men were reminiscing again. I could tell the older guys were getting tired because there weren't as many of them in the lobby as there was the night before. I went to sleep.

Sunday, October 29, 1995

The meeting began at 8:00 am. A man who was introduced as the president of an organization called Negro League Baseball Players Association, Association got up and greeted us. He said it was great having everyone here and that there was some unfinished business he wanted to take care of. Many of us had never heard of the association before this day but it appeared that they represented us as an entity. I found out later that the association had been formed several years earlier in New York with a former Negro League player named Wilmer Fields as president.

As the meeting went on, a question came up before the association about an announcement that Major League Baseball Commissioner, Fay Vincent, had made a few years earlier regarding medical insurance for all Negro League players. In a largely publicized decision, Vincent had ordered the major leagues to provide all Negro League baseball players and their wives with the major leagues' medical plan. He would do this through a man named Len Coleman, who worked in the accounting office of the major leagues.

65

January 4, 1993

Dear Mr.

Attached please find your Negro League Medical Plan
information book and enrollment form explaining the
coverage. If you wish to enroll, please tear out the
enrollment form on the inside cover of the last page and
return the completed form in the self-addressed envelope
enclosed.

If you have any questions, please call the toll free number,
1-800-992-8354, extension 520.

Sincerely,

Leonard S. Coleman, Jr.
Executive Director
Market Development

350 Park Avenue. New York. NY 10022 (212) 339-7800

65

Introducing A Winning New Medical Plan

Major League Baseball is introducing a winning new Medical Plan, effective May 1, 1993, for former Negro League ballplayers and their wives.

If you are eligible, the Medical Plan can mean money in your pocket by helping to pay hospital and doctors' bills if you or your wife are sick.

Major League Baseball pays the full cost of your new Medical Plan coverage. But you have to sign up. Fill out the card on page 11 of this booklet. Tear it off and mail it in the enclosed envelope. You don't have to put a stamp on it; we've done that for you.

2

When Len Coleman got the order from Vincent, he in turn asked a friend of his who had played in the Negro Leagues to help him find all the living Negro League Players and notify them about their eligibility to be insured under the major league medical plan. Coleman would then issue application forms to all the former players and their wives.

His friend was Joe Black (Baltimore Elite Giants). Joe Black was here at the reunion with us in Kansas City and was coincidentally the vice president of Baseball Assistant Team (BAT). BAT is a charity organization that helps out former major league baseball players and others who were associated, if they need assistance with extenuating circumstances in their lives. BAT works closely with the major leagues.

I was curious as to why I had not received an application for the medical insurance. I looked around me at the sad state many of my colleagues were in and wondered if they had received an application. We didn't have medical insurance back when we played ball. We were very dependent on the game. Sometimes we played two or three games a day, and if a guy had a broken bone he played on it or he wouldn't get paid. I still limp from the break I sustained during my ball playing days. It ended my major league career that had not just begun. That's the way it was back then. It was the way we lived because our choices were few. Based on the humming in the room, I surmised that I was not the only person who did not receive an application.

The president of the association said that letters regarding the insurance were sent out and that we would have to contact Joe Black regarding the insurance issue. He then quickly introduced the spokesperson for Major League Properties, a marketing group for the major leagues. This bothered me because as the representative of us ball players, I felt the association should have spoken up for us and gotten all of us applications right then and there.

The spokesperson for Major League Properties said nothing about insurance. However, she did say that they had secured authorization from the Negro League Museum in Kansas City, Missouri to make licensing contracts with organizations around the country that wanted to produce and sell Negro League memorabilia.

I could feel some excitement in the room but I was a little confused. Why would they go to the museum for authorization to sell on our behalf? Wouldn't they need to go to the organization that represented us – the association? Maybe the museum represented us. After all, they were the ones that were instrumental in bringing us together this weekend. But if the museum represented us, then who was the association and in what capacity did they represent us?

The spokesperson went on. She said that all players of the Negro Leagues were to receive a royalty check from Major League Properties resulting from the sales income this new licensing agreement would generate. This sounded great to some of the players. Too many players were forced to live in squalor after they could no longer play ball. They had to sell most or all of their Negro League memories for cash to live on and for medical care in their older years, so this was wonderful news to them.

"Most of them are poor. They didn't take Social Security out of the money we made while we were playing.
—Sherwood Brewer

The spokesperson continued by saying that the royalties would result in the profits being divided up with a payment of thirty percent to the Negro League Museum in Kansas City, Missouri, twenty percent to the Jackie Robinson Foundation, and fifty percent to be split by all the living members of the Negro Leagues. I was a bit disconcerted by this. I felt that all the profit of any sales with Negro Leagues on it should go to these old men, and as they pass on it should benefit the organization that represents us, which ever one it was.

Others however, were visibly excited by this pronouncement. There was a great deal of chatter in the room and then opinions started to fly about who should receive the royalty money. Several older players stood up and said the Negro League ended in 1947 and that anyone who played before Jackie Robinson didn't have a chance to play in the majors and anyone after Jackie did, so the Negro Leagues officially ended when Jackie Robinson broke the color barrier. Therefore they demanded that those who played after Jackie Robinson shouldn't be able to reap the benefits of those royalties.

That reasoning seems to be popular even today, however, those who came after Jackie experienced just as much discrimination as before Jackie. Remember, it took more than ten years to fully integrate major league baseball, and even then only half the teams had more than one minority playing. After Jackie broke the color barrier, there was rumored to be another gentlemen's agreement: No more than two minorities on a team. Jackie may have been credited for opening the door but if you read up on baseball, most Blacks that were accepted in the majors were accepted with only semi-open arms. That proverbial open door was not really open all the way until July 21,1959 when the last major league team to integrate, the Boston Red Sox hired Elijah "Pumpsie" Green. And just because the door was open, that didn't mean everyone had a chance. Discrimination and politics were still at work for years to come.

The discussion at the meeting quickly became heated between the younger players and the older guys. It was argued that some very notable players were too old to move into the major leagues when Jackie broke the barrier and it had been a necessity for them to keep playing in the Negro Leagues, if they were to continue receiving a paycheck.

There was also the fact that even after Jackie Robinson, many great ballplayers weren't called by the major leagues until they proved themselves in the Negro Leagues, Willie Mayes, Ernie Banks, and Hank Aaron included! The ensuing argument was nearly out of control when Buck O'Neil finally ended it by standing up and saying, "We're going to have a vote!" Buck O'Neil was again acting as a spokesperson for all of us.

The vote was 210-8 against 1947 being declared the end of the Negro Baseball League. Mr. O'Neil then proclaimed that any player that played on a Negro League team between 1947, and 1960, the last time anyone remembers a Negro League game being played, was considered a Negro League ball player and would be eligible to reap the benefits of membership just as those who played between 1920 and 1947. There was cheering among the assembled players.

The next question was about how we would receive the royalty checks. The spokesperson for Major League Properties said that she had ordered the association to furnish a list of all eligible Negro League players to Major League Properties and they would send checks to those on that list.

This was very disturbing to me because the Association had been around for nearly five years and most of us had never heard of them. Most had also never heard from them, so we knew that the Association had no idea how many of us there really were or where we lived. How were we to receive anything if the Association didn't know we existed?

That comment ended the meeting. We were told to check out of the hotel and get on the buses to the airport. We left for our buses thinking we were all members of this Negro League Ball Players Association since that was the only organization known to us that represented us, and that we would all be getting royalty checks in the future because we had all played for the Negro Leagues.

The buses were ready. We went to the airport but we left there confused. There were a lot of questions not answered about the medical insurance or the list that the Association had that they were going to give Major League Properties for royalty checks. Something was not right and I felt strongly about finding out what was really going on.

At the airport I saw 74-year-old Sherwood Brewer (Kansas City Monarchs) with 93-year-old Bobby Robinson (Detroit Stars). It was as if a force drew us to each other. I approached Mr. Brewer and asked him about the medical insurance. Mr. Brewer made a statement to me that he had never gotten a letter about insurance from the major leagues and Mr. Robinson said the same. That was confusing, because they had both played for the Negro Leagues for more than a decade and both had played before Jackie Robinson was signed to the major leagues! Surely someone knew they were still around. Why wouldn't they have gotten a letter about the insurance?

Although I had a pension and insurance, many of these old men had nothing. This started me thinking about what I could do to get the names of all the players and get them signed up for the medical insurance and the royalty checks. I discussed the matter with Mr. Brewer and he gave me his telephone number in Chicago saying he would help me in any way he could.

Sherwood Brewer early years

CHAPTER THREE
A Conspiracy Uncovered

I didn't realize how a seemingly minor task could become so complicated. All I needed to do was get the names of all the living players to the right place to get them signed up for the medical insurance. I called the Major League office and asked what insurance company represented the major league players. I eventually found out that Travelers Insurance wrote the insurance policy. I contacted an underwriter at Travelers Insurance and innocently requested insurance application forms for the Negro League ballplayers who did not get them. The lady who answered the telephone told me that she couldn't give out any application forms unless Joe Black approved it first.

I called the Major League offices again, this time asking for Joe Black. He was not available so I asked to be transferred to Len Coleman. After all, Len Coleman was the person who was ordered by the Commissioner to find all of us. He was not available either but he did call me back later that day and politely told me that since Joe Black was a colleague of his who had played in the Negro Leagues, he called on him to help locate the living players over a six-month period. When Mr. Black found all the names he could from the Negro Leagues for the medical insurance plan, they closed it out.

I explained that we lived all over the country and that six months wasn't enough time to locate the more than two hundred of us that might qualify for the insurance. At that, Mr. Coleman asked me when and for what team I played. I told him that I had played for the Chicago American Giants in 1953 and 1954. At that point, Mr. Coleman started to get very arrogant and said that any player after Jackie Robinson didn't count because they had a chance to play in the majors. I said that was not true because there were a lot of players that were too old to go in, and a lot of people who came after Jackie.

Before I could tell him about the vote we had at our reunion, he said, "Too bad, they still had a chance to go to the major leagues and this is why they are not getting the medical insurance." Then he hung up the telephone on me.

They claim that this League went out of existence in 1950. That's a total lie. This League just gradually died. There isn't a legal document nowhere in this country that declared that League dead. It just died. People are going around telling people the League went out of existence in '50. It did not. It just died out... I'm one of the few that played on both sides of '50 so I know who was out here, so they're leaving a lot of guys out. They want to cut (it) off to 1947 so you know who they're leaving out? They're leaving out three Hall-of-Famers! Ernie Banks, Henry Aaron, and Willie Mays! Can you imagine? Not that they need it; they don't need it, but it's just the principle of the thing.
—Sherwood Brewer

Undeterred, I called Joe Black. Joe Black was the Vice President of BAT and since Mr. Black had played in the Negro Leagues, I felt that he would be sympathetic and helpful. Mr. Black told me that he had already closed the offer. I asked him why and he said he had found all the living players that he could only over a six-month period and that he closed the offer after that. I told him that I found all the living players he missed and that he should open it back up. He said, "No." I said, "That is not fair. We've got over two hundred people still living out here that need this medical insurance." I asked him who gave the order to close it out. He merely said he found all the players he could find. Then he said, "It's too late... I closed it," and he too hung up the telephone on me.

> "Our biggest enemy is some of our own people who went along with them when all this was organized a few years ago, just for profit. Some of our worst enemies are our own people; our own ball players"
> —Sherwood Brewer

I was appalled. How could one of our own do this to us? He was at the reunion. He knew that we all agreed that anyone who played through the 1960 season was considered a Negro League ball player. Someone else must have made him stop trying to locate the players for the insurance. Certainly he wouldn't do this to us if given a choice. I had to find another way to get those insurance applications.

> "It was inexcusable for Joe Black to say that he couldn't locate all the ball players because mouth-to-mouth, it could have been done mouth-to-mouth but what they did, they just cut it off too soon. Too lazy or didn't care, as long as they got it and a few of their friends and just forgot the rest of us. So it's been a sad thing."
> —Sherwood Brewer

At that moment I ended my investigation. I was very frustrated. This was not fair. I realized that to get what the players deserved I'd have to get with the organization that represented us and go through them. We would need to band together as one voice and go back to the major leagues and tell them that we voted and that we are all eligible and we want that medical plan for some of these people before it's too late. They need it.

> "At this point I don't need it but I will need it one day and when it does come I want to be eligible to receive it. And I'm going to fight to get it for the rest of the guys that are still living today that really need it."
> —Dennis Biddle

I called the Director of Major League Properties. Although she was in charge of the royalty checks, I though she might be able to help. She suggested that the Association could use some young blood and thought that if I wanted to get anywhere with my mission, I should call them and ask them to become their president-elect. I called the Association and spoke to the president of the organization. I asked him if I could be a part of the organization as their president-elect and get all of the ball players organized and get them the benefits they deserved. He said, "That's a good idea." I told him I'd be back in touch with him and we hung up the telephone.

My mind was racing. I had our representing organization backing me now but knew we still needed some outside help. We needed to get some legal advice on how to get to the bottom of this mess and find out why so many of the living players hadn't gotten any applications for the insurance, why so many of us were left out, and why it was closed out so quickly. It seemed ridiculous to me that everyone was so closed-mouthed about the whole situation. I didn't know where to go because I knew the Association had little money, but I also knew that something needed to happen, and soon.

Shortly after the reunion I received a letter from the Museum in Kansas City and as fond memories of our reunion ran through my mind, I opened the envelope. The letter was to inform the Negro League ball players that the museum no longer represented us and that we should go to the Association for any benefits or concerns we may have in the future. I called Mr. Brewer. He had gotten a letter too. We discussed the letter and wondered why the museum would use their authority to release our licensing memorabilia rights to the public and then drop us like this. The only thing we could think of was that they wanted the money associated with Negro League memorabilia but not the responsibility of representing us. I was disillusioned by this whole state of affairs.

"The museum is there to preserve our history and I am very appreciative of that but there are a lot of things that are going on there that are not conducive to the needs of the players today. A lot of money is being raised using our name, using the Negro League as a means of raising funds, but none of the players are getting any of the money raised. A lot of letters go out to major organizations for fund raising efforts saying they represent us, but they don't. They are not doing things fairly. We got a letter after the 75th reunion saying that they no longer represented the players and that we should go to the Ball Players Association but two years later they are still using us as a way of soliciting firms for their gain. There is nothing wrong with that but there are 250 men living out there—give them some of the recognition and compensation for their hard work over the years to make the Negro League a name worth funding."
—Dennis Biddle

"The major league ball clubs are decent to us but the problem is with the museum and an organization that was organized about seven years ago and we feel that all they have done is use us to raise money. None of it comes back to us and we think that is very unfair. There's nothing wrong with the museum but how about doing something for guys while they're alive? That's more important. We'd like to see some of that money they take in trickle down to our ballplayers."
—Sherwood Brewer

OF THE NEGRO BASEBALL LEAGUES

October 27 - 29, 1995
Kansas City, Missouri

Lester *Buck* Lockett
Carl Long
Earnest *The Kid* Long
Lee *Lucky* Mabon
Raydell *Lefty* Maddix
Enrique *Lefty* Maroto
Frank *Lefty* Marsh
Edward A. *Marty* Martin
Verdell *Lefty* Mathis
Nathaniel *Nath* McClinic
Clinton *Butch* McCord
Walter *Mac* McCoy
James *Big Jim* McCurine
Ira D. McKnight
Clyde *Junior* McNeal
John *Mule* Miles
Ray Miller
Jessie James *Mitch* Mitchell
John Mitchell
Robert *Peach-Head* Mitchell, Sr.
Lee *Big Man* Moody
James Robert *Red* Moore
Constance E. *Connie* Morgan
Emilio *Milloto* Navarro
Orlando *Chico* O'Farrill
Warren *Dadd* O'Neil
William J. *Stein* Owens
Willie *Pat* Patterson
Warren *Bill* Peace
Maurice *Babyface* Peatros

James Pendleton
Art David *Superman* Pennington
Norris *Playboy* Phillips
Richard *Dick* Phillips
Jose *Potatoe* Piloto
David *Buckey* Pope
Willie Pope
Andrew Porter
Merle M. *Fancy Dan* Porter
William *Bill* Powell
Henry *Hank* Presswood
Marvin D. *Thumper* Price
Ted *Double Duty* Radcliffe
Ted R. *Skiper* Rasberry
Ulysses A. *Hickey* Redd
Eddie Lee Reed
Harry *Lefty* Rhodes
Charles L. *Charlie* Rivera
Henry Frazier *Slow* Robinson
James *Jim* Robinson
William Bobby Robinson
Bienvenido *Benny* Rodriquez
Tommy *Sammy* Sampson
James *Jake* Sanders
Carlos Santiago
Jose Santiago
Augustus Saunders
Joseph *Scotty* Scott
Joseph Burt *Joe B.* Scott
Robert *Bob* Scott

Edward *Scottie* Scott, Sr.
Eugene *Dick* Scruggs
Barney *Grillo* Serrell
Robert *Pepper* Sharpe
Arthur Lee *Big Art* Simmons
Hubert V. *Bert* Simmons
Herbert Harold *Herb Briefcase* Simpson
Eugene *Smitty* Smith
Quincy Smith
Taylor Smith
Willie Smith
Alvin Spearman
Joseph B. *Bullet* Spencer
Riley Stewart
Alfred *Slick* Surratt
Earl *Micky* Taborn
Ron *Schoolboy* Teasley
James *Lefty* Turner
Thomas *High Pockets* Turner
Eli Underwood
Bill *Billy* Van Buren
Armando Vasquez
John Walker
James *Bo* Wallace
Johnny Washington
Price West
Ernest *Tennessee* Westfield
Eugene *Stanky* White
Davey L. *Wiz* Whitney
Leonard D. *L. D.* Wiggs
Jimmy *Seabiscuit* Wilkes
Eli Williams
Eugene *Fire Ball Willie* Williams
Jesse S. *Bat Man* Williams
Larry Williams
Robert *Bobby* Williams
Wallace *Bucky* Williams
Willie *Curley* Williams
Al *Apples* Wilmore
Artie *Smiley* Wilson
John E. Wilson
Bill *Wild Bill* Wright
John *Buffalo* Wyatt
Willie Young
Jim *Zipper* Zapp

Go with picture with (over) Players ON Field.

75TH ANNIVERSARY
OF THE NEGRO BASEBALL
LEAGUES

October 27 - 29, 1995
Kansas City, Missouri

"LIST OF ATTENDEES"

Robert *Ab* Abernathy
George *Jo-Jo* Altman
Hipolito *Torrento* Arenas
James *Jimmie* Armstead
Jesse Askew
Russell Awkard, Sr.
Otha *Little Catch* Bailey
Sam Barber
Mrs. Joe (Willella) Barnes
William Barnes
Herbert Barnhill
Bill Bell
Gene Benson
William *Fireball* Beverly
Dennis *Bose* Biddle
Dan Black
Joseph *Joe* Black
Jim *Fireball* Bolden
Lyman Bostock
Frank *Dick* Bradley
Luther *Lu* Branham
Ollie Brantley
Bill *Chip-Chest* Breda
Sherwood *Woody* Brewer
Clifford Brown
William *Cap* Brown
Sidney Bunch
Ernest Burke
James *Jim* Carter
William *"Ready"* Cash
James *Fireball* Cohen, Sr.
Cecil *Cole* Cole
Elliott *Junior* Coleman
Eugene *Rip* Collins
James *Fireball* Colzie
Leroy *Cro* Cromartie
Charlie *Lefty* Davis
Ross *School Boy* Davis
Mrs. Leon (Geraldine) Day

James *Jimmy Dean* Dean
Felix *Felle* Delgado
Wesley *Doc* Dennis
Carl Dent
Clifford *Cliff* DuBose
Claro Duany
Mahlon *Duck* Duckett
James *Big Train* Dudley
Frank Duncan
Melvin *Buck* Duncan
Lacy Ellerbe
Frank Evans
James *Dean Blue* Everett
William *Billy* Felder
Albertus *Cleffie* Fennar
Leroy *Toots* Ferrell
Wilmer *Chinky-Bill* Fields
Ed *Mike* Finney
Hiram *Lefty* Gaston
Robert *Rab-Roy* Gaston
John *Bay* Gibbons
Walter Lee Gibbons
Josh Gibson, Jr.
Louis *Seaboy* Gillis
Stanley *Doc* Glenn
Herald *Bee Bop* Gordon
Harold *Hal* Gould
Willie Grace
Whit Graves
Chester *Popeye* Gray
Wiley Lee *Diamond Jim* Griggs
Felix *Felo* Guilbe
Napoleon *Nap* Gulley
Raymond *Ray* Haggins
Harold *Buster* Hair
Sam Hairston
Arthur *Junior* Hamilton
Lovell *Big Pitch* Harden
Charles *Chuck* Harmon

David *Rough House* Harper
Ernest *Oink* Harris
Lonnie Harris
Willie *Red* Harris
Wilmer *Will* Harris
J.C. Hartman
Sammie *Sam* Haynes
Albert *Buster* Haywood
Neal *BoBo* Henderson
Joe *Prince* Henry
Francisco *Pancho* Herrera
Ulysses *Slim* Hollimon
Gordon *Hoppy* Hopkins
Herman *Doc* Horn
Henry *Hen* Howell
Cowan *Bubba* Hyde
Monford *Monte* Irvin
Elbert *Issy* Isreal
James *Sap* Ivory
John *Loopie* Jackson
James *Pee Wee* Jenkins
Byron *Mex* Johnson
Clifford *Connie* Johnson
Don *Groundhog* Johnson
Ernest *School Boy* Johnson
Joshua *Josh* Johnson
Ralph *Big Cat* Johnson
Thomas Johnson
Walter Johnson
Mamie *Peanut* Johnson-Goodman
Clinton *Casey* Jones
Cecil Kaiser
John Kennedy
Edward Kimball
Henry *Kimmie* Kimbro
Larry *Schoolboy* Kimbrough
Willie *Bill* Lee
Rufus *Lu* Lewis
Anthony *Tony* Lloyd

It's funny how things just fall into place sometimes. That only means it was meant to be.

Dennis Biddle

I had been working as a volunteer at the Community Youth Development Center at this time and they had asked me to speak at a young adult gathering about the Negro Leagues and my involvement.

Two days later, I found myself speaking about the history of the Negro Baseball Leagues and I mentioned my new role with the Association as their president-elect. I told them how I was going to involve myself in finding out what happened to the medical insurance for some two hundred people who had not been contacted for the benefit. Although this endeavor seemed straightforward enough, I knew from my recent experience that it would be difficult at best to get this undertaking accomplished.

A young photographer named Sy White was hired to photograph me at the gathering. After my speech, Sy approached me and told me he had someone he wanted me to meet who might be able to help me with my problem. He told me he would set something up and to meet him at the Athletic Association on Wednesday morning at 11:00 am.

I met Sy on Wednesday morning and he introduced me to a man named Martin J. Greenberg. Mr. Greenberg is a noted sports attorney in Wisconsin. We chatted for a short time and then Mr. Greenberg asked me to meet with him in his office the next morning.

After arriving at his office, I revealed to Mr. Greenberg the plight of many former Negro League baseball players. I described the frail state that many of my former teammates were in and the dishonorable conditions in which many must live after giving their life to the game of baseball. I explained how we did not have Social Security, a pension, or medical insurance back then.

I told him how we were promised medical insurance from the major leagues and how that wasn't happening for many of the former players, even some of those who played during the ridiculous time frame criteria for benefits that Black and Coleman had apparently set up. I told him what I had done thus far to remedy the situation and the obstacles I had faced in trying to do so.

Then I recounted the meeting that took place at the 75th reunion and the vote we had regarding the Negro League and when it officially ended. I told him we agreed, as a ballplayer's organization, that anyone who played for the Negro Leagues should reap the benefits of being a part of that League. I told him that Joe Black from BAT and Buck O'Neil from the Museum were there and knew that, but did nothing with the major leagues to remedy the situation.

Then I told him about the letter we got from the museum separating itself from any affiliation with us and about the organization, the Negro Leagues Baseball Players Association, that the museum stated was the recognized organization to represent the living players.

I revealed the deal that was in the works to sell the licensing for merchandise with Negro League on it and how each entity would benefit. I also told him that I felt any profits from the sales of anything saying Negro League should go back to the living players because it was our sweat and our hard work that made us legends and it is our past and our history that makes any item with Negro League on it worth purchasing in the first place. I told him that I didn't think we should have to share the profits with any organizations that don't represent us because it is obvious that they do not care about the well-being of the players themselves.

I explained how various people and organizations are using our name, Negro League, and making a lot of money off of it because the owners of our League did not preserve it. I also explained how a few individuals from the Negro Leagues have made a career for themselves but that the majority of the former players really needed to ban together to get the medical insurance benefits as promised, and the opportunity to profit off of the millions of dollars spent each year to buy Negro League memorabilia.

"We were in New York about three years ago to a celebration and in the New York Times…up to that point there was 2.4 billion dollars had been made from Negro League memorabilia over the past 5 years and we got none of that. Now a lot of people out here who have contributed, really thought money was coming to us because we'd been told by a lot of people who contributed, but it never reached us. The museum and a couple of organizations around the country sucked it up and it never reached us. And I'm very disgusted about it."
Sherwood Brewer

Dennis "Bose" Biddle and Sherwood Brewer

Mr. Greenberg listened intently and eventually took our Negro League case pro bono. He started to unravel the confusion by calling the State of Maryland where the Association's office was located. It was then that he uncovered the fact that the Negro League Baseball Players Association was filed under two individuals' names, not the name "Negro League" as we all had assumed.

This meant that the organization did not represent us at all! The organization that Major League Properties, the Museum, and the ball players thought was supposed to represent the Negro League ball players, actually only represented the interests of two people, its owners. The two men who owned the Charter were the only ones who would benefit from anything. It also meant that the rights of the living players of the Negro Leagues were not really represented either! I couldn't believe what I was hearing.

I called the president of the Association immediately and told him what we had discovered but he became very condescending and said he would "look into it" and hung up the telephone. I was astonished!

After more investigating, we discovered that the Negro League Baseball Players Association was a group that claimed to have about one hundred members. They worked on a play for pay basis. The only beneficiaries, with few exceptions, were elderly former players who could travel to card shows. In the past, there had been public allegations that some of the players were not being paid their royalties and that "certain personnel converted money." There was "no accountability with respect to funds generated" and "investigations" had been conducted "into the business of the organization by the District Attorney's office of New York" (*New York Times*, March 15, 1993). We also learned that BAT had criticized the organization repeatedly.

It was at this time that I knew that I needed to do something on behalf of the living players but I did not know exactly what I was going to do. After talking with Sherwood, we decided to start with Major League Properties. I called the Assistant Director at the Major League Properties to tell her what we had discovered about the Association. I told her that the Association was not representing the Negro League and that two unknown men were behind it to benefit, not the living players. She asked how I knew this and I told her about Mr. Greenberg's investigation into the charter in Maryland. I then told her that I was going to look into starting an organization that did represent all the living players since the Association didn't. I was feeling a charge of energy when I said this. I said we could then work with Major League Properties on getting those royalty checks to all the former players.

I called Mr. Greenberg again for guidance and he said the first thing we needed to do was to get a charter together representing *all* the living Negro League players right away, before it was too late. I provided Mr. Greenberg with a list of former ball players that I had obtained from a historian in Kansas City and when he asked me how many players would sign an affidavit, I referred him to the man I had talked with at the airport, Sherwood Brewer. Mr. Brewer seemed to know just about everyone from the League and when Mr. Greenberg called Mr. Brewer in Chicago and asked how many men Brewer felt he could get to sign affidavits, Mr. Brewer said, "All."

Mr. Greenberg organized the papers for affidavits and a charter to be filed in the State of Wisconsin, which would represent all the living players of the Negro Baseball League. His document explained that since the owners of the Negro Baseball League didn't preserve our history or the name, it went to the public. That is how these two men in New York were able to get a charter to make money for themselves, by using the Association as a front.

DENNIS BIDDLE

ARTICLES OF ORGANIZATION
OF
YESTERDAYS NEGRO LEAGUE BASEBALL PLAYERS, LLC

83

These Articles of Organization are executed by the undersigned for the purpose of forming a Wisconsin Limited Liability Company under Chapter 183 of the Wisconsin Statutes.

Article 1. Name of Limited Liability Company is <u>Yesterdays Negro League Baseball Players, LLC</u>.

Article 2. The street address of the initial resigstered office is:

<u>330 East Kilbourn Avenue, Suite 925</u>
<u>Milwaukee, Wisconsin 53202</u>

Article 3. The name of the initial registered agent at the above address is: <u>Dennis Biddle</u>

Article 4. Management of the limited liability company shall be vested in:

(X) a manager or managers.
OR
(   ) its members.

Article 5. <u>Name</u> and <u>complete address</u> of the organizer:

Dennis Biddle
9418 North Green Bay Road
Brown Deer, Wisconsin 53209

Dated: *April 22* , 19 *96* .

(Organizer signature)

This document was drafted by: Attorney Martin J. Greenberg.
330 E. Kilbourn Ave., #925
Milwaukee, WI 53202

FILING FEE — $130.00

Return acknowledgement to:
Martin J. Greenberg
State Bar No. 01013746
DEUTCH & GREENBERG
330 E. Kilbourn Ave., #925
Milwaukee, WI 53202
(414) 271-9958

SEC-STATE
I.D. #

Y002233

101

THE STATE OF WISCONSIN

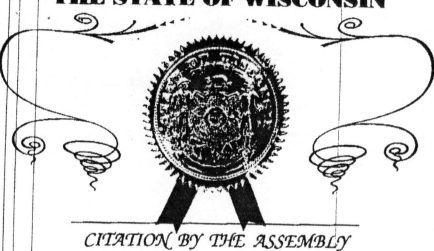

CITATION BY THE ASSEMBLY

KNOW YOU BY THESE PRESENTS:

WHEREAS, in 1953, Dennis Biddle at the age of 17, became the youngest player in the Negro Baseball League as a member of the Chicago American Giants; and

WHEREAS, in June of 1953, Dennis Biddle outpitched Philadelphia Stars player Lefty McKinnis, one of the few men to ever beat Leroy Satchel Paige; and

WHEREAS, Mr. Biddle became known as "The Man Who Beat the Man Who Beat the Man"; and

WHEREAS, Mr. Biddle's promising career as a ballplayer in the Negro Baseball League and aspirations to follow Jackie Robinson into the major league were prematurely cut short by a broken ankle, and

WHEREAS, since Dennis Biddle retired from baseball he has devoted his life to helping young people turn their lives around; now, therefore,

Representatives Spencer Coggs and Antonio Riley on behalf of the Wisconsin State Assembly, with the concurrence of Representatives Johnnie Morris–Tatum, Robert Turner, A. Polly Williams and Leon Young, and Senators Gary George and Gwendolynne Moore, under Assembly Rule 97, hereby commend Dennis Biddle for his outstanding service to the Negro Baseball League and the youth of Milwaukee, and congratulate the Negro Baseball League on the occasion of its 75th Anniversary.

Representative David Prosser, Jr.
Speaker of the Assembly

STATE CAPITOL
MADISON, WISCONSIN

March 7, 1996
Date

Representative Stephen Freese
Speaker Pro Tempore

DENNIS BIDDLE

13

DFI/CCS/Corp
Fm 3 (7/96)

United States of America

State of Wisconsin

DEPARTMENT OF FINANCIAL INSTITUTIONS

September 19, 1996   CORP I.D.# Y002257

CERTIFICATE OF INCORPORATION
of

YESTERDAY'S NEGRO LEAGUE BASEBALL PLAYERS FOUNDATION, INC.

The STATE OF WISCONSIN hereby grants to said organization
the powers and privileges conferred upon it by Chapter 181 of
the Wisconsin Statutes, for the pursuit of any purpose lawful
under said Chapter, except as may be further limited in its
articles of incorporation.

IN TESTIMONY WHEREOF, I have
hereunto set my hand and affixed
the official seal of the Department
on the date above written.

Richard L. Dean, Secretary
Department of Financial Institutions

ANNUAL REPORT   Corporations formed under Ch. 181 of the Wisconsin Statutes are required to file an annual
report with the Department of Financial Institutions.

Form to Use   DFI/CCS/Corp Form 17.   Blank report forms are mailed to the corporation, c/o its registered agent
at the agent's address on record with the department, and are distributed during the calendar quarter in which
the report is due.

When to File   The DUE DATE is fixed by the calendar quarter within which the organization was incorporated.
If, for example, the incorporation date is May 26, the due date for the report is the last day of that quarter,
June 30.

Where to File   By mail, to WISCONSIN CORPORATION ANNUAL REPORT, at the address indicated on the report form, or
at the department's office at 30 W. Mifflin St, Madison.

REGISTERED AGENT and AGENT'S ADDRESS   Each corporation is required to continuously maintain a registered agent
who resides in Wisconsin. The initial agent and agent's address were set forth in the articles of incorporation,
but may be changed by filing a written change statement with the department. Request DFI/CCS/Corp Form 113 from
DFI, P O Box 7846, Madison WI, 53707, or make the change in the space provided on the annual report form.

The above requirements are statutory, and further, it is important that the agent and agent's
address be kept current, as annual report forms, notices and other official communications
are directed to the corporation through its registered agent on record with the department.

REPORTING REQUIREMENT FOR CHARITABLE ORGANIZATIONS THAT SOLICIT CONTRIBUTIONS   Notice is hereby given, pursuant
to s. 181.32(2), Wis. Stats., that a NONSTOCK, NONPROFIT corporation engaged as a charitable organization and
soliciting contributions, is subject to reporting requirements with the Wisconsin Department of Regulation &
Licensing, pursuant to Ch. 440 of the Wisconsin Statutes. Please call or write for further information and
filing requirements to: WISCONSIN DEPARTMENT OF REGULATION & LICENSING, Attn: Charitable Organizations,
P O Box 8935, Madison WI, 53708. Phone (608) 266-0829.

- Printed on Recycled Paper -

We decided to call our organization Yesterday's Negro League Baseball Players. Because of the misconception that former players would benefit when the public buys something with the words "Negro League" on it, the word "Yesterday's" was added to our Charter. This would protect the living players and separate Yesterday's Negro League Baseball Players from any other organizations claiming to represent the living Negro League players. It would also serve to link us as one united force and not separate individuals trying to accomplish the same thing.

Assuming the president and ball player members of the illegitimate charter would want to abscond that charter, the papers we were going to send out had the president of the association listed as president, and my name (Dennis Biddle) listed as president-elect of our newly named organization. Fifteen affidavits went out of Mr. Greenberg's office. Then I received a phone call from the president of the Association. He said he did not want his name put on anything sent out of Greenberg's office. This confused me but there was no time to waste so we changed everything on the affidavits to read Dennis Biddle as president and Sherwood Brewer as vice president and sent out the remaining affidavits. Thus we had begun our foundation.

In order to develop programs for the best interests of the living players, we formed two organizations. The first was Yesterday's Negro League Baseball Players, LLC. This would be a limited liability company which would enable us to raise public awareness, seek enshrinement for worthy members in the National Baseball Hall of Fame in Cooperstown, New York, act as a spokesman for the members with respect to any third-parties, generate monies to create a fund to benefit members in ill health and financial straits, and with prior written consent of its members, to use their names, images, autographs, etc. to generate income that would be shared among the members, after expenses were paid.

The other organization was the Yesterday's Negro League Baseball Players Foundation, Inc. The goal of the foundation would be to preserve the history of the living players and those in Halls of Fame, and to set up educational programs to perpetuate that preservation.

During this time, I received a call from the assistant director of Major League Properties telling me that the two men who owned the Negro League Baseball Players Association (NLBPA) were getting ready to take over all licensing for the Negro League. I told her that I had already set up an organization to legally represent the living Negro League players and that they could now go through us to get the players their royalty checks. She told me that whatever I was going to do to stop them, I had better do it quick.

So I called Mr. Greenberg again and he faxed the assistant director of Major League Properties a copy of the Yesterday's Negro League Baseball Players charter and sent a letter to notify her that we are now the legal representatives of all the living players in the charter. Now, anyone who wanted to work with the former players of the Negro League for any reason could go to the one organization that represented all of them. She ignored us. She never responded.

DENNIS BIDDLE

First Check received From MLBP. INC.

MAJOR LEAGUE BASEBALL PROPERTIES

July 29, 1996

Dear Former Negro Leagues Player:

We are pleased to enclose a check in the amount of $69.26. which represents your share of royalties received from Major League Baseball Properties' Negro Leagues licensing program for the period of December 1, 1995 through May 31, 1996. We apologize for the delay in getting it to you and for any inconvenience we may have caused.

Currently, our roster of licensees includes 22 companies that are dedicated to our program and continue to support it. From the date of inception through the above mentioned closing date, the program has generated a total of $261,225 in royalties. We have distributed 100% of this amount to former Negro Leagues players (50%), the Negro Leagues Baseball Museum in Kansas City (30%) and the Jackie Robinson Foundation (20%). We are very proud of the results of our program and look forward to continued growth.

As you know, Major League Baseball Properties administers this program on a pro-bono basis. We do not deduct any expenses from the royalties collected. During the past year, we have launched several initiatives to promote awareness for the Negro Leagues at our expense. Last February, we negotiated a deal with Wheaties to produce a Negro Leagues commemorative cereal box. The box featured Satchel Paige, James "Cool Papa" Bell and Josh Gibson. The promotion marked the first time that any member of the Negro Leagues was featured on a Wheaties box. In May, we exhibited at Black Expo USA in New York. We invited several local former Negro Leagues players to take part in the event and we sold licensed products. In coming months, we plan to launch a national trade advertising campaign and a retail catalog to further promote the program.

In December, 1996, we will send you another check representing your share of royalties we collect from June 1, 1996 through November 30, 1996. Should you have any questions regarding the Negro Leagues licensing program, please feel free to call me at 212-339-8452.

Sincerely,

Deidra K Varona
Licensing Supervisor

DKV:tbm

cc: D. Gibson
       C. Dunn

350 Park Avenue, New York, NY 10022 (212) 339-7900 http://www.majorleaguebaseball.com

A few weeks later, we received over one hundred fifty applications from Negro League players across the country who wanted us to represent them in our quest.

It was about this time that Mr. Greenberg received a letter from a Maryland attorney named Charles Winner (May 29,1996). In his letter, Winner stated that he represented the NLBPA and acknowledged the fact that we were starting an organization to represent the players. He attached a list of their current members, many of them already deceased, accused us of creating an organization to rival the NLBPA, and claimed that we were using names of some players without their permission. He also mentioned the possibility of issuing a license to our group to make and sell Negro League products but that we would have to go "through the Association's nominated exclusive agent, Major League Properties."

Mr. Greenberg responded with a letter (June 12, 1996) confirming the establishment of the Foundation and outlining the purposes of our organization. Along with it, he sent a copy of the Articles of Organization for the Foundation. He noted that several names on Winner's list of members, who supposedly assigned sole rights to the Association, were also Directors of Yesterday's Negro League Baseball Players. Greenberg asked Winner for copies of any agreements signed by the players, giving proprietary rights to their name and likeness, for the exclusive use of the Association. He also asked for their Articles of Organization. Several letters were sent to Winner asking for this documentation, however, Mr. Greenberg never received a response.

P. 2

87

Law Offices of
Deutch & Greenberg

Suite 925
330 East Kilbourn Ave.
Milwaukee, WI 53202
(414) 271-9958
(414) 271-2329 FAX

Alan H. Deutch, S.C.
(Court Commissioner)
Martin J. Greenberg

Of Counsel:
Harvey J. Goldstein

Legal Assistants:
Lennie A. Braczinski

Paralegals:
Karen Klett
Sandra Trester

June 12, 1996

Atty. Charles S. Winner
Fisher & Winner
VIA: Fax - (410) 727-1362

RE: Negro League Baseball Players, LLC

Dear Mr. Winner:

Unfortunately, because of my absence from the City, I was unable to respond to your letter of May 29, 1996, sooner.

You correctly stated that Yesterday's Negro League Baseball Players, LLC has been formed and is a limited liability company in good standing with the State of Wisconsin. The purposes of the organization are:

1. The Association shall advance the public interest and the knowledge and understanding of the Negro Baseball League and its teams and players.

2. The Association shall seek enshrinement of all worthy members of the Negro Baseball League to the National Baseball Hall of Fame in Cooperstown, N.Y.

3. The Association will act as a spokesman for its members and represent its members with respect to any and all third-parties.

4. The Association will generate funds through sponsorship, licensing, autograph sessions and other forms of promotions to create a fund to benefit members in ill health and financial straits.

5. The Association, with the prior written consent of its members, shall utilize the names, images, signatures, autographs and likenesses of its members to promote the Negro Baseball League and its players with the purpose to generate income, which income, after the payment of expenses, shall be shared among the members.

LAW OFFICES

FISHER & WINNER, LLP

SAMUEL J. FISHER (1886-1971)
ALAN H. FISHER, JR. (1922-1994)
CHARLES S. WINNER
LOUIS I. KAPLAN
CAROL L. RUBIN
GERARD KING STEVENS *
STUART LEVINE
ROBERT B. LEVIN

ERIC M. NEWMAN
LAUREN EVERS McCOMAS **

OF COUNSEL
HOWARD I. GETLAN
DAVID W. BRITTON, JR.

BETTY D. YOST-PRESSER
PARALEGAL

* ALSO ADMITTED IN D.C.
** ALSO ADMITTED IN VIRGINIA

315 NORTH CHARLES STREET
BALTIMORE, MARYLAND 21201-4325
(410) 385-2000
FAX (410) 727-1362

TOWSON OFFICE
401 WASHINGTON AVENUE, SUITE 900
TOWSON, MARYLAND 21204-4806
(410) 823-0173

WASHINGTON AREA OFFICE
6001 MONTROSE ROAD, SUITE 301
ROCKVILLE, MARYLAND 20852-4817
(301) 585-3444

May 29, 1996

VIA CERTIFIED MAIL, RETURN RECEIPT REQUESTED

Martin J. Greenberg, Esquire
Deutch & Greenberg
330 East Kilbourn Avenue
Suite 925
Milwaukee, WI 53202

      RE: Yesterday's Negro League Baseball Players, LLC

Dear Mr. Greenberg:

      I represent the Negro League Baseball Players' Association (the "Association"). It has come to our attention that your client Dennis Biddle intends to start an association of Negro league baseball players under the name of "Yesterday's Negro League Baseball Players, LLC" to rival the Association.

      This letter is to put you and your client on notice that players including those on the attached list have granted to the Association the <u>sole and exclusive rights</u> to use their name, signature and likenesses, including the rights to use any photographs and artistic renditions of their likenesses, under a group licensing program, as you are possibly unaware of same. As you are planning to institute a group licensing program in conjunction with your group, you are hereby advised that the Association intends to vigorously protect the property rights already granted to it by the players.

      The Association would be willing to discuss with you the possibility of issuing a license to your group so it can legitimately make and sell products bearing the names, likenesses or signatures of these players. This must be done through the

Mr. Charles S. Winner
June 12, 1996
Page 2

In your letter of May 29, 1996, you indicate that:

> "This letter is to put you and your client on notice that players including those on the attached list have granted to the Association the <u>sole and exclusive rights</u> to use their name, signature and likenesses, including the rights to use any photographs and artistic renditions of their likenesses, under a group licensing program, as you are possibly unaware of same."

On the list as attached to your May 29, 1996, letter, are names of certain members of your organization which are also Directors of Yesterday's Negro League Baseball Players, including James A. Dean, Herman "Doc" Horn, Joshua Johnson, Verdell "Lefty" Mathis, Merle Porter and Jim Zapp.

Would you please be so kind, at your earliest convenience, to fax me a copy of any signed Agreement bearing the names of the afore-referenced wherein they have granted to the Association the sole and exclusive rights as previously referenced.

I am enclosing a copy, for your review, of our Articles of Association. Would you, likewise, be so kind as to tender to us a copy of your Articles of Association.

I feel it would be fruitful, in that our joint interest is the best welfare of members of the Negro League, to discuss areas of mutual interest and concern and therefore, your suggestion to open the line of communications relative to our two (2) groups I feel is most beneficial.

Thank you for your expected cooperation.

Sincerely,

DEUTCH / GREENBERG

Martin J. Greenberg

MJG/mf

87

FISHER & WINNER

May 29, 1996
Page 2

Association's nominated exclusive agent, Major League Baseball Properties.

I caution you not to act in contravention of the licensing rights already granted to the Association by the players. The Association will be substantially and irreparably damaged should this occur. If you have done so already, you must cease and desist all production, distribution and/or sale of any such products immediately. The Association will institute legal action against your client for any unauthorized use in contravention of its property rights, interference with the Association's contractual relations and any other appropriate claim. These proceedings may not be limited to injunctive relief, but may also include monetary damages to the extent possible.

I have also been advised that some of the players' names set forth in the Yesterday's Negro League Baseball Players, LLC Members' Agreement and otherwise are being used without the permission or authority of the players. Any unauthorized use of the names of any players is to cease immediately.

Please avail yourself of this opportunity to avoid any unpleasant legal proceedings. Should you have any questions or wish to discuss this matter, please contact me directly.

Very truly yours,

Charles S. Winner

c: Wilmer Fields, President
Major League Baseball Properties

F:\WPDOCS\LAUREN\BASEBALL\BIDDLE\GREENBER.001

"We've been had. Over the course of about ten years we've been had by a lot of people, mainly the museum and another organization that we had once and Major League Properties. Course I don't blame Major League Properties too much because they only done what they were told to do). Their job was to handle the money that came in from the Negro League Black memorabilia and they did. But what happened when we organized, they should have worked with us but they didn't. They continued to work with an organization that never really existed. We had been supporting a non-existing organization and we caught them. Our lawyer caught them. But they still ignored us."
—Sherwood Brewer

A few weeks later, I heard from the Assistant at Major League Properties again. This time she called to tell me that the two guys who had the charter for NLBPA in their names finally pulled the charter and had inexplicably disappeared. I was delighted. I felt my first taste of success with that news. I felt that Major League Properties would now know to come to Yesterday's Negro League Ballplayers Foundation if they wanted to work with the organization that represents all the former players of the Negro Leagues. Then I realized that this left the president of the Association in a helpless situation because he now no longer had the backing of a charter. I wondered what he would do next.

I didn't have to wait long. I received notice that the former president of the association had filed a new charter. He filed it under the name of Negro League Ballplayers Association (NLBA), again known as the Association and that this charter organization was set up as the successor to the NLBPA (the former "Association"). Now their organization was legitimate however, it seemed there were two organizations competing with each other to represent the interests of former Negro League players; one that benefited older players (the Association) and one that would benefit all the players, Yesterday's Negro League Ballplayers Foundation (YNLBPA).

Fortunately, our charter for Yesterday's Negro League Baseball Players had already been filed so we had the legal right to represent and protect the rights of the former Negro League baseball players that signed the affidavits. Unfortunately, this would also separate us as a united force and weaken the power of both organizations.

If we would come together as one, we would be a force to be reckoned with.
—Dennis Biddle

A letter went out from the NLBA, the Association dated December 13, 1996. In the letter it stated that there was confusion in the past about who would receive royalty checks from Major League Properties. It stated that the distribution of royalty checks for December 1996 and in the future would be determined by membership, or lack thereof, with the Association. The letter stated that they were dividing its membership into Full Members and Associate Members, depending on when they played in the Negro Leagues. We believed that their membership was only around seventy at that time, but it was not substantiated.

First and only check received from MLB P Inc.

DOBIAS PTG., L.I.C., NY 11101

VENDOR No. 006081

MAJOR LEAGUE BASEBALL PROPERTIES INC.

CHECK No. 078165

| 12/96NLROYALTY | 12/13/96 | 1674 | 191.87 | 12/16/96 |

191.87

REMITTANCE ADVICE

191.87

MAJOR LEAGUE BASEBALL PROPERTIES INC.
350 PARK AVENUE
NEW YORK, NY 10022

CHEMICAL BANK
11 WEST 51 STREET
NEW YORK, NY 10019

| NUMBER | DATE | AMOUNT OF CHECK |
| 078165 | 12/16/96 | $*******191.87 |

VOID 6 MONTHS FROM DATE OF ISSUE

No. 078165

1-12
210

PAY **ONE HUNDRED NINETY ONE DOLLARS AND 87 CENTS**

006081   DENNIS BIDDLE
TO   9418 N. GREEN BAY ROAD APT#211
THE   BROWN DEER, WI 53209
ORDER
OF

MAJOR LEAGUE BASEBALL PROPERTIES INC.

That meant if a former player did not sign on with their organization, they would not receive a royalty check. I had received royalty checks up to this point in time but because I did not want to join their organization, my checks stopped. And so did the checks of anyone else who did not join. A lot of guys signed up just so they could receive their money! This is how they built up membership in their Association.

I felt that it was very unfair to force people to join the Association in order to get paid. I called Major League Properties again and they said my name wasn't on the list the Association provided to receive royalty checks. I explained that the assistant director had a letter and documentation from our attorney that proves we are the representatives of all the former players and we should be the ones supplying a list to them, not the Association. The man on the other end said that the assistant director of Major League Properties was no longer employed there and that he was just doing what he was told.

Since Major League Properties was still acknowledging the Association as the recognized representatives of the players and getting a list of players from them instead of from our organization it was obvious that there must have been something going on between the two groups that undermined our authority to speak for all of the players. It was sad that we were so divided but I knew their charter wouldn't help most of the living players, so we pressed ahead with our efforts.

12k

WISCONSIN SPORTS AUTHORITY LUNCHEON
'BASEBALL LEGENDS OF THE NEGRO LEAGUE'
July 21, 1999
Martin J. Greenberg

Every great journey begins with courage, perseverance, and enough strength to overcome whatever roadblocks lie ahead. Today, we acknowledge those characteristics in the men, and a league that are as integral to baseball as Abner Doubleday. Without the Negro Leagues, the story of baseball would be incomplete.

The first Negro League was started in 1920 because men of color were not permitted the opportunity of playing in the major leagues due to the infamous 'gentlemen's agreement.' This agreement prevailed for 47 years, until Jackie Robinson was signed by the Brooklyn Dodgers in 1947. With the walls slowly falling, more African Americans were admitted into the major leagues and in 1960, the Negro Leagues ended. The Negro Leagues refer to various leagues during the years 1920 - 1960, including the Negro National League; the Eastern Colored League; the Negro Southern League; the Second Negro National League; the Negro American League; and others.

Many African-American ballplayers began their careers in the Negro Leagues and then moved into the majors. Several of the brightest of these transitional black stars now have plaques at the Baseball Hall of Fame in Cooperstown. Among them are

Satchel Paige; Monte Irvin; Roy Campanella; Ernie Banks; Willie Mays; Hank Aaron; and Jackie Robinson.

Today, less than 250 men who played in the Negro Leagues are still living, and many are without adequate medical coverage and financial assistance.

Honoring these five players today is an affirmation of their role in developing the game of baseball. Their efforts, talents, skills, and determination, coupled with grace, confidence, and a love for the game, took baseball into the 20th century. It is impossible to appreciate the great African-American athletes of today without paying tribute to those individuals who were the trailblazers, and the pathfinders to the future. They were the barrier breakers of baseball.

They challenged the boundaries of everyday existence. They contested habitual norms. They explored a new realism and relationships. They erased the limits of convention. They made the American Dream more accessible to all." The African American ballplayers who composed the Negro Leagues were trailblazers whose glory, courage, and stamina have had a resounding impact on modern day sport.

One can neither cheer nor scorn current players without acknowledging a time in American history when the rules of the game were dependant on the color of one's skin. These pioneers gave the greats of today an opportunity to participate in the game on an equal playing field.

Yesterday's Negro League Baseball Players have made it their goal and purpose to not only promote and benefit the living players of the Negro Leagues, but to continue the process of education about the Negro Leagues, so that America never forgets the hardships that befell the early African-American ballplayers. It is their commitment to present a constant reminder that as Americans--regardless of race--we are one under the law. The sport of baseball, and human compassion, are far greater than skin color and ignorance. It is their commitment to ensure that we never forget the struggles endured by the past, which paved the road to the present.

CHAPTER FOUR
Yesterday's Negro League Ball Players Foundation

O ur goals for the Foundation were many. We wanted to get the medical insurance most of us had not received from the major leagues. In order to do that, we needed to get to the bottom of the issue with Joe Black and Len Coleman.

"We have men up to ninety-five-years-old and none of them got that insurance and that's shameful. That's a disgrace. We have one, Bobby Robinson (ninety-four years old). He came to this league with its inception. And they tell me they didn't know about him? I can't buy that one."
—Sherwood Brewer

Because we didn't get a pension from our ball playing days, we also wanted to set up some kind of plan so the guys could get some money coming in on a regular basis.

These guys are in their 80s and 90s and they can't get social security. They only get a little old folks (check) that they can get, and they're barely making it on it -and they are living legends! These are the guys who struck out Josh Gibson and hit home runs off of Satchel Paige and people have forgotten about them and the people who have played with them and claim to represent them
have forgotten about them."
—Sherwood Brewer

We wanted to educate the public, not only about the history of the Negro Baseball League but to reveal the fact that there are legends who played in the Negro Baseball Leagues still living today! And, if anyone wanted to reach us, they could do so without having to go through the museum. We also wanted to let the public know that the only organization that truly represents and supports the former Negro League players themselves is Yesterday's Negro League Ball Players.

We wanted to get formal recognition for the living players of the Negro Leagues for being such an important part of baseball history, including the women who played with us in the Negro Leagues.

So we started an organization called YNLBPA to represent all the players in that played in the Negro League. Our efforts will help everyone realize a gain, not just one or two of the lucky ones who can get speaking engagements arranged for themselves.
—Dennis Biddle

Finally, we wanted to develop our foundation in such a way that it would continue to benefit people long after we Negro League players are gone. In essence, we wanted to leave a legacy.

I knew I could not spread my energy into all of these areas at once. I would need to set up the organization first and let others help me with the rest, so I put my faith in the Lord and went to work trying to get a bunch of us together to form the internal structure of the foundation. I decided to start looking for assistance in my hometown. Since I had a continuing rapport with the Milwaukee Brewers, I contacted them and asked for their help. I sent a letter telling them what I was trying to do. My thought was that if the Brewers could help bring twenty men to Milwaukee, the men could help me set up the foundation's internal structure. Then we in turn, would make a field appearance at Milwaukee County Stadium during a Brewer game and sign autographs for the fans. It sounded like a fantastic arrangement that would benefit everyone involved. The Brewers agreed.

I invited twenty Negro League players to Milwaukee for two days to help Sherwood and me set up the office of our organization. Mr. Greenberg and Mr. Eisenberg, another local attorney, were present to help form our structure and to give us advice. During our meetings in those two days, the board of directors was voted on and set up. Mr. Sherwood Brewer was named vice president of the organization and I was named president. A secretary and a treasurer were also named, as well as some other vice presidents.

"Some marketing and some money has fallen to players but now they have someone who can speak for the living."
—Martin Greenberg

During that weekend, when we weren't working on the set-up of the organization, we signed autographs before, during, and after the Brewer games. We also signed autographs at Legends, a sports restaurant in downtown Milwaukee. They sponsored an autograph-signing session at their establishment for us. A local radio station also sponsored a breakfast and a live show to help us spread the word about our foundation and its mission.

Baseball fans were able to meet some of the greatest ball players of all time and in turn, we were able to get some help setting up the organization. More importantly, we were able to get some local recognition for the Negro Leagues. All in all, I think it was a big success.

With the weekend over and the foundation set up, it was our hope that individuals and other companies would donate money to help fund our organization. Unfortunately so many other groups claimed to represent the Negro League ball players, it was hard to get anyone to donate. Sherwood Brewer and I went to several big businesses in Wisconsin for possible donations including Miller Brewery, Coca-Cola, and many others, but because they had all given donations to the museum in Kansas City, they felt that they had done their part to help and declined to give more. We found that because Buck O'Neil was well known as a former Negro League player and manager, and worked at the museum, it was assumed by most everyone we approached that the museum in Kansas City was our executive agent.

Even though we explained that the museum preserved our history only and did not represent us and did nothing to help the living players themselves, we still couldn't get any donations. The public was under the impression that the museum was there to represent the living players and the museum didn't seem to be stepping forward to state otherwise.

"All the promoters around the country, people who want to invite us to card shows and things like that, they are under the impression they have to go to the museum and that isn't so. The museum has succeeded in making people think they have to go to them to get us for an appearance and they do not. We can go whenever we want to with whoever we want to."
—Sherwood Brewer

"And when they do go through the museum to get a representation from the Negro League there is very few men that the museum recommends all the time."
– Dennis Biddle

"The museum got so strong, once, about their authority over us that they would open our mail! People who wanted to write to us and didn't know our address, they would write to the museum. [They] would open our mail. [They] opened mine once but [they'll] never do it again. So, we've been taken. We've been had. Over the course of about ten years we've been had; by a lot of people, mainly the museum and another organization that we had once. No one's making money at that museum it seems, but Buck O'Neil. He's cleaning up. -Sherwood Brewer good word for us. I believe in my mind that the reason that Don Motley who runs the museum fights so hard to get personal appearances for Buck O'Neil is because he and Buck O'Neil is splitting the pot! I told them so, and I just made up my mind. I am going to fight them as long as I live because they're just using us and that's it, and then they forget us."
—Sherwood Brewer

"The museum could step up in ways to help the ball players better than what they are doing. They're not saying anything about what's happening to us. It is though they don't even care that it is happening, but yet we are the reason they are there!"
Dennis Biddle

After several attempts to acquire donations from across the country, we realized that no one knew who we were as an organization so we had no credibility. We knew now that before we could ask for money we had to gain recognition as a bona fide foundation. That meant we had the monumental task of separating ourselves as an entity apart from the museum and other satellite organizations that claim to represent us.

Being up against such competition was difficult at best. We had no money coming in so the only way to keep the office running was to put ourselves on public display. Since Mr. Brewer and I were retired and could travel freely, we decided to take to the airways and railways, signing autographs and talking about our history in order to spread the word about our plight.

We talked on the television, the radio, and in person at several speaking engagements around the country. We went to colleges, universities, high schools, middle schools, and grade schools trying to enlighten young people about the Negro Baseball Leagues and to keep our history alive. It was very exciting to speak to the younger generation because we knew that the history of the Negro Leagues was vague, at best, to them and this would help to keep our true history alive. It was very gratifying because we were able to discuss events that even their parents couldn't tell them about. As I spoke, I looked into the faces of these young people and I wished that someday someone would care enough to investigate our history further and take charge of continuing to share it with the next generation when we are gone. I have received many letters from students around the country in the various schools where I spoke. Each letter is dear to me and is a symbol of the appreciation of my work and the importance of the history I can share.

While traveling throughout the country, we also went to shopping malls and military bases to share our history. We were given space in the mall to talk about the history of the Negro Leagues and to sign autographs. We had found that many people had seen the museum before but did not know the true situation, so we had to explain our role versus the museum's role. As we signed hundreds of autographs, we talked to as many people as possible about the Negro Leagues and why we had to organize ourselves. Even though we received donations through these efforts, our expenses far exceeded the small donations we obtained.

I was speaking to some guys at an Army base about the Negro Leagues and one of them said his great grandparents used to own a Negro League team but they didn't know a lot about it. This was very interesting because these guys were White, and this confirmed for me what my friend had told me so many years ago about the true owners of the Negro Leagues being White.

Then we found of a way we might be able to make more money. We had a company make some T-shirts for us and when people made donations of twenty dollars or more, we gave them a shirt and an autograph. This seemed to work well so we also had some hats made and we used this venture to keep the office running until we could get enough money from other sources to run the organization effectively. A graphic company made some baseball cards for us to give out to fans too. We could always get a donation for our card and an autograph.

Three years after Sherwood Brewer and I had traveled the country spreading our history and the word about our plight, some of the other Negro League players had heard about what we were trying to do and offered to help us. We were excited. We set up a program where any former Negro League player who was a member of our organization could go out and talk about our history. The foundation would give them a stipend in exchange for an autograph session at shopping malls and military bases in the area in which they lived. They could give out memorabilia and autographs, for donations, while talking about their experiences in the historical Negro Leagues. Half of the money received would go to the players involved and the other half would go to the foundation. This way the players who couldn't traveldue to age, illness, or other reasons, would still reap some type of benefit from the event.

We felt this would work out well because it would allow former players to receive personal recognition for their contributions to the Negro Leagues while helping other players. It would also help the foundation stay afloat at the same time.

"Some of us is always going to something. Were always being invited to something

but it's always the same guys. Isn't that strange? It shouldn't be that way. I just tried to give up two of my invitations so someone else can go…I've been before. Why invite me? Invite some of the younger guys that's never been. That's the way it should be. I called and tried to trade with someone, they wouldn't let me. We have guys that have never been invited to a card show. They look out for their favorites and we're trying to do something about that. I'm real bitter. I'm terribly bitter."
—Sherwood Brewer

Although these efforts helped to gain recognition for the foundation, after awhile the expenses as a whole once again exceeded what we were making. The cost of the memorabilia alone exceeded the money being made and all too soon we had gone into a lot of debt to the vendors who furnished our products. We decided we could only send one guy at a time to an autograph session instead of four or five. This helped a lot. For five years we set up these autograph signing sessions and we still do it to this day.

With Sherwood Brewer's help, I recommitted myself every day to finding different ways to get donations and recognition for the foundation, and find money making ventures for the living players. My hope was to have something established in every city where a Negro League player lived. That way each of us could leave our mark on society and in our community in a positive way. We had already started an annual golf outing in Wichita, Kansas, and set up a scholarship fund to honor players from Wichita.

KANSAS MINORITY BUSINESS DEVELOPMENT COUNCIL

The Kansas Minority Business Development Council
Welcomes you to the

3rd Annual

Bob Thurman Golf Tournament

May 16, 2003
WSU Braeburn Golf Course

With Special Guest...

Yesterday's Negro League Baseball Legends

We found that trying to keep the foundation alive was a true effort. While we wrote letters to the major leagues about the on-going medical insurance issue, we traveled the country to seek recognition and to fight for our right as former Negro League players to represent ourselves. We sought out ways to help our players through donations and fundraising events. There were a lot of ups and downs. Most of the time there were more downs than ups. Although we met a lot of good people along the way, the vast majority had mostly empty promises and selfish intentions. I had trusted people with various books, memorabilia, valuable papers, and documents they would need to assist me, but then never heard back from them.

I tried not to let it devastate me when I was lied to or intentionally taken advantage of, but it grew wearisome over time. I was also notified on a regular basis of players' deaths. Players were dying that couldn't afford to be buried. Players who were instrumental in helping me with the work of the foundation were also dying. I couldn't help feeling like I wasn't working fast enough or hard enough. I began to feel powerless, and very alone. I often found myself wanting to just give it all up. After all, I certainly didn't intend on having to deal with the political foolishness that surrounded this whole medical insurance matter with the major leagues. I also didn't expect it to be such an effort to get any answers to my questions regarding the medical insurance. Besides, I had medical insurance and a pension. So many times I felt that all this unwarranted stress in my life was unnecessary.

It was about this time that rumors started to surface about my role in the Negro Leagues. Some people started accusing me of never playing for the Negro Leagues. This was not only insulting but it was very demoralizing. I had received a commendation from the State of Wisconsin for my contributions to the Negro Leagues. I was also read into the Congressional Record on February 27, 1996 as being the youngest player of the Negro Baseball Leagues, and now even some of our own players were trying to discredit me! It was very disappointing.

It seemed that someone wanted me to stop doing what was in all of the players' best interest. Perhaps someone was uncomfortable with the questions I was asking and with what we were uncovering. Perhaps someone had other plans for monies that were generated for the Negro Leaguers and our efforts were interfering with their individual interests or revenues.

It was times like these I was glad to have Sherwood Brewer on my side. Sherwood always encouraged me to keep going. His message to me was always about pressing forward and fighting for what was right, no matter what the personal cost. He would tell me, "You're gonna find out that some of your own is your worst enemy. They gonna talk about you and discourage you in many ways but I want you to press on to the mark."

Then he would say to me, "You watch the organization and I'll watch your back."

"They take a shot at Dennis because they're trying to protect their own turf."
—Martin Greenberg

Sherwood never talked about what a great second basemen he was when he played in the Negro Leagues. He never bragged. He only talked about what a gratifying experience it was for him and how he felt he was treated fairly by the fans and how he was grateful to be able to forget the past wrongs and press on toward the future. "If there's something in the past that is hindering you," he would tell me, I want you not to dwell on it, but keep pressing on toward the things that will make our organization strong and that will benefit those in the League who are still alive."

I continued to try, but despite the passionate and encouraging words of Mr. Brewer, it would soon prove to be a futile effort. The time finally came when we couldn't afford much of anything. At one point, we had to decide whose telephone to keep connected, Mr. Brewer's or mine. Mr. Brewer felt that since I was the president of the foundation that mine should stay ringing, so we disconnected his. We had no money other than my retirement money and Sherwood Brewer's retirement money to go on the road to try and keep the foundation alive. So, that is what we used. Some places we went to we barely got expenses met. Sherwood and I couldn't afford to sleep in a motel until we made enough donations signing autographs to pay for the room. Many times we had to sleep in the car while we were on the road and we joked about this. It brought back memories of our ball playing days in the Negro Leagues. Back then, there were many times we had to sleep on the bus because we weren't allowed to sleep in the local hotel. Although most of the time we had kept our sense of humor and an optimistic outlook on our situation, many times I found myself asking if it was worth all the effort. And of course, if I ever mentioned something to Mr. Brewer about it, he would encourage me and give me the strength to keep going.

He helped me understand that I could not let anything stop me from continuing my efforts and that I could not allow myself to falter despite any setbacks or obstacles I would have to overcome. This was way too important to our future. It was not just about me and how tired I felt or what may have happened that day or week to diminish my ambitions. It was about all of us who played for the Negro Leagues. It was about principle. It was about what was right and what was wrong. It was right that we all deserve the medical insurance that was offered by the major leagues and it was wrong to leave so many of us out of the deal. It was right that we should all receive the profits from the sales of our memorabilia too. And so we continued forward.

> "Fortunately I'm one of the older guys so I will probably benefit off of everything but that isn't the way I want it. I want everybody to share. Dennis is one of the young ones. He's going to miss a lot of things because he came later."
> —Sherwood Brewer

Then, just when I thought we were done for again, we finally got our first substantial donation. One team player, Jimmy Dean, donated one hundred shares of his Merck stock to the foundation before he passed. Jimmy Dean was a good friend of Sherwood's and an awesome pitcher for Philadelphia Stars in the Negro Leagues. We decided we would the stock to help finance the business end of the foundation. We turned the stocks around and immediately invested them into Dean Whittier. I felt a bit more secure knowing we had this money in our trust.

CHAPTER FIVE
Empty Political Promises

In 1997, two years after the formal organization of our players, we were still at an impasse concerning the medical insurance issue with the major leagues. Although Faye Vincent had ordered Len Coleman to offer former Negro League players major league medical insurance, and we had written letters to the major leagues regarding the issue, most of us were still without. It was beginning to seem like they were purposely ignoring our pleas, perhaps due to political reasons.

Everything seemed to be politically motivated these days. I had received royalty checks from Major League Properties until we filed for the foundation's charter. After that, I no longer received checks. Mr. Brewer's assistance from BAT was cut off several times and he was still not recognized for the medical insurance, even though he qualified.

One day, I heard word that United States Senator Carol Moseley-Braun of Illinois asked the owner of the Chicago White Sox to revive a proposal to give Negro Leaguers a pension. Bud Selig, acting baseball commissioner, presented the idea at the Arizona owners' meeting for approval. The idea was for the major leagues to set up a pension fund for former Negro League ballplayers funded through donations from the owners and the Major League Baseball Players Union. Ms. Moseley-Braun thought this pension could serve as a kind of reparation for the wrongs that had been done in the past by keeping Blacks out of the major leagues. This was not the first attempt to give former Negro Leaguers a pension but it would at least put it back on the table for discussion. The proposal was presented and this time the owners agreed that it was a good idea to start a pension for all the former Negro Leaguers. They asked the Major League Baseball Players Union to participate as well, however, they declined.

Len Coleman, who was now President of the National League, was also present at the meeting in Arizona. Somehow during the course of the meeting, Coleman managed to assume the responsibility of making sure that these pension funds were distributed to the Negro League players.

"I can't understand why the President of the National League would take it upon himself to represent us former Negro League ballplayers when Yesterday's Negro League Ballplayers foundation was already organized and legally represented the players at that time. He knew that."
—Dennis Biddle

"No one is speaking up for the players but two guys in the main office up there who have no business speaking up for us. One of them is Joe Black who played in the Negro League. He is the assistant to Joe Garagiola who runs the Baseball Assistance Team

organization. The other guy is Len Coleman who is now President of the National League. These two guys are calling themselves representing us. And we don't feel that's right."
—Sherwood Brewer

Instead of contacting Yesterday's Negro League Baseball Players organization, the organization that represents all the former players, to set the criteria, to get a list of living players from us, or to find everyone around the country that may have qualified, Len Coleman once again called on Joe Black and once again they set up their own special criterion to determine who would get the pension and how they would get it.

It was decided that in order to receive the pension, one would have to have played in the Negro Leagues for a minimum of four years before Jackie Robinson. This meant that only thirty-six living players out of over three hundred who should have been eligible would qualify. Included in that number was Joe Black and a small list of players that he seemingly knew and liked.

It was very frustrating that no one bothered to consult with us about the pension or the criteria. Even more frustrating was that no one who in a position to do so, i.e., Buck O'Neil, the former player who worked in a highly-public position for the museum or Joe Black, former player who worked in a high-up position with BAT, the organization that works closely with the major leagues, would speak up for our rights.

Chicago Sun-Times **BASEBALL**, Monday, January 20, 1997   73   107

Negro Leaguers to get pensions

BY JOE GODDARD
STAFF REPORTER

Baseball clubs moved Sunday to create pensions for former Negro League players and for surviving major-leaguers who didn't play beyond 1947.

Sam Jethroe, the National League's Rookie of the Year in 1950, heads the known list of eligible players, most of whom are now in their 80s. Each will receive between $7,500 and $10,000 a year once he shows proof of service time.

Sen. Carol Moseley-Braun (D-

Ill.) revived the pension idea two months ago with a call to White Sox chairman Jerry Reinsdorf, who in turn asked acting commissioner Bud Selig to present it to the executive council at the ownership meetings last week in Scottsdale, Ariz.

The owners hope the players union will participate, too, but they aren't counting on it.

"I would hope they would have the integrity to pitch in, but [union aide] Gene Orza said not too long ago that it would be 'unseemly to help those people,' whatever that means," Reinsdorf

said. "I talked to Bud about it, and he said, 'To hell with the union. If they don't want to do it, we should do it ourselves."

"I think it's great that the clubs are going to rectify their discrimination against blacks that they practiced all these years," Orza countered.

Jethroe, who has fallen on hard times, hit .273 with 18 home runs, 100 runs scored and 35 stolen bases for the Boston Braves in his rookie season, but he was back in the minors less than three years later.

Contributing: *Associated Press*

Country Club to overtake Mark   ...vecchia, who now has   ▶ Tournament scores

Negro Leaguers gain pension plan

Major League Baseball, saying it wants to right a wrong, will fund a pension plan for Negro Leaguers and other pre-1947 players.

Under the plan, 1950 National League Rookie of the Year Sam Jethroe is among 90 former Negro Leaguers who are eligible to receive $7,500-$10,000 annually. Jethroe, 75, had sued owners, claiming discrimination kept him from qualifying for a baseball pension. The suit was dismissed Oct. 4.

The plan, which could cost $10 million, covers players with at least four years of service in the Negro Leagues or combined service in the ma-

jor and Negro leagues. It also will benefit about 100 players who were in the majors before baseball's pension began in 1947.

"We cannot restore the careers of the Negro Leaguers, but ... the very least baseball can do is to provide a pension," National League President Leonard Coleman said.

MLB wants the players union to contribute, too. Union head Donald Fehr said Sunday that he didn't have enough information to comment.

By Chuck Johnson
▶ Ivan Rodriguez's record pact, 13C

UROPEAN EDITION AND USA TODAY ASIA & PACIFIC EDITION WHEN

USA TODAY   1/20/97

Mrs. Gwinn to this date most of the Players have not received one dime. 10,000,000. was Donated.

We are the only organization that represent all the players. how Joe Black, Lynn Colman took over for us will never know, and nothing is being done about it.

JB

"I think they [the museum] should do more to recognize us, to help us. They should step up. It is my understanding that the Major League has offered us a pension and they are having some problems with it. And the problem they are having is the players, who's qualified and who's not. If Buck O'Neil would step up for us we'd get a lot done but he will not do it, so that means he doesn't care. Buck was one of the most respected ballplayers among us. Every ballplayer in the country liked Buck. And he turned on us. Buck O'Neil has forgotten us. [He] has absolutely ignored us. I played for him and with him. He was my manager, when Ernie was with him, Ernie Banks. And you never would have made me believe that Buck O'Neil would forget us. But he has. He's making good money and he's just forgotten. Like I said, the Negro League ball players have been had by a lot of people, and some of our own."
—Sherwood Brewer

Within a short time, pension payments were in the works and checks were being sent to a few of the former players. Mr. Brewer and I filed a grievance with the Major League Baseball commissioner on behalf of all living players of the Negro Leagues. We felt that the responsibility of setting the criteria and finding all the eligible players should have gone to the foundation that spoke for the players (YNLBP), not to a couple of men who did not represent us and who apparently had ulterior motives. We protested that any decisions regarding the money provided for our pension should have gone to the organization that represents the players. That way we could apportion it to all the players, not just a select few.

This was the second time that most of the former players of the Negro Leagues would be purposely left out of a benefit that they should have been able to receive from the major leagues.

Mr. Selig asked us for legal documentation of our foundation proving that we were the legal representatives of the living Negro League players. We promptly supplied him with the documents and he said he would turn them over to the owners. A short time later, the pension payments stopped. We figured that when the owners received the paperwork and noticed that YNLBP legally represented the players, the major leagues stopped the pension payments in order to settle the issue of who actually represents the living players, and perhaps wanted that organization to handle the disbursements of the pension.

Law Offices of

Deutch & Greenberg

Suite 925
330 East Kilbourn Ave.
Milwaukee, WI 53202
(414) 271-9958
(414) 271-2329 Fax

109

Alan H. Deutch, S.C
(Court Commissioner)
Martin J. Greenberg

Of Counsel:
Harvey J. Goldstein
Richard R. Sindic

Legal Assistants:
Monica A. Ford

Paralegals:
Sandra Trester

February 7, 1997

Mr. Bud Selig, Commissioner
Major League Baseball
c/o Milwaukee Brewers
P.O. Box 3099
Milwaukee, Wisconsin 53201

Dear Commissioner Selig:

I have been retained by and represent Yesterday's Negro League Baseball Players, L.L.C., and Yesterday's Negro League Baseball Players Foundation, L.L.C., a Wisconsin limited liability company and a Wisconsin non-profit, non-stock corporation, Dennis Biddle, President.

The first Negro League was started in 1920 because *men of color* were not permitted the opportunity of playing in the Major Leagues due to the infamous *'gentlemen's agreement.'* The gentlemen's agreement came from a Congressional ruling *"The Jun Crow Law,"* used by Major League owners to keep men of color from playing on their Major League teams. This agreement prevailed for forty-seven (47) years until Jackie Robinson was signed by the Brooklyn Dodgers in 1947. With the walls slowly falling, more blacks were admitted into the Major Leagues, and in 1960 the Negro Baseball League ended. For purposes of this letter, the "Negro League" shall refer collectively to those leagues that were first started in 1920 and which lasted through 1960 and include, but are not limited to the Negro National League, Eastern Colored League, Negro Southern League, Second Negro National League, Negro American League and any other leagues that were color oriented during the afore-referenced period, i.e., 1920 through 1960.

Today, less than three hundred (300) men who played in the Negro League are still living. Many people and organizations have expressed a desire to help these players financially and otherwise. In truth, these players helped to form and build organized baseball into the sport that it is today. Despite this fact, very little help has been received by the majority of the players who are still living. Many of the remaining Negro League

Mr. Bud Selig
February 7, 1997
Page 2

players are in their 90's, 80's and 70's, with a few in their 60's. The majority of these players are living without adequate medical coverage and financial assistance.

There are several groups that claim that they represent or have represented the players of the Negro League.

The Negro League Baseball Museum, Inc., is a not-for-profit organization, organized under the laws of the State of Missouri and located in Kansas City, Missouri. John Buck O'Neil, a former Kansas City Monarch first-baseman, is Chairman of the Negro League Baseball Museum. The Museum, besides admissions, generates income from licensing. It was estimated in a March 15, 1993, article in the New York Times, that the Museum had 14 licensees whose products yielded an estimated $6 million in retail sales, which, obviously, the Museum received a percentage in royalties. The Museum's sole intent is to raise money to perpetuate the history of the Negro League. The Museum does not provide money to former Negro League players. Copies of the By-Laws of the Negro League Baseball Museum is attached. (Attachment 1)

Negro League Baseball Players Association, Inc., a New York non-profit, non-stock corporation was organized in 1990 by Richard Berg, a music producer, and Ed Schauder, a lawyer. This group's stated purposes were to (By-Laws attached as Attachment 2):

* Sponsor programs and events providing financial assistance to its members;

* Seek enshrinement of worthy members into the National Baseball Hall of Fame;

* Expand the Negro League exhibit in Cooperstown;

* Provide personal support through fraternization of its members;

* Sponsor educational programs on the Negro Leagues;

* Sponsor youth programs and little league programs in the inner cities in memory of Negro Leaguers;

* Document and preserve the history of the Negro Leagues.

Mr. Bud Selig
February 7, 1997
Page 3

It's Board of Directors and President were:

President	-	Monte Irvin
Board of Directors	-	Richard Berg, Jim "Mudcat" Grant, Monte Irvin, Ferguson Jenkins, Willie Stargell, Max Manning, Lionel Hampton, John "Buck" O'Neil, Billy Williams

The real objective of the Negro League Baseball Players Association, Inc., was "to get money to the players now" through licensing deals, card shows and events. This organization utilized Leisure Concepts as its agent for licensing deals. The group, which claimed to have 100 members, claimed the right to market the faces of 100 Negro League Players and was a "play for pay" organization. With few exceptions, the only beneficiaries were those elderly former players who could travel to card shows. The organization folded in 1996 amidst allegations that the players were not paid royalties, that certain personnel converted money, that there was no accountability with respect to the funds generated and investigations into the business of the organization by the District Attorney's Office of New York.

We believe that the successor to the Negro League Baseball Players Association, Inc., is a group now known as the Negro League Ballplayers Association, a Maryland corporation, which we believe was established by a Maryland attorney named Charles S. Winner of Fisher & Winner, LLP, 350 North Charles Street, Baltimore, Maryland, 21201-4325.

In May of 1996, I received a letter from Atty. Winner, in essence, indicating that he was putting the undersigned and Yesterday's Negro League Baseball Players on notice that "...players, including those on the attached list, have granted to the Association sole and exclusive rights to use their name, signature and likeness, including the rights to use any photographs and artistic renditions of their likenesses, under a group licensing program..." (Attachment 3) On June 12, 1996, the undersigned wrote to Atty. Charles Winner asking for a copy of any signed agreement bearing the names of certain individuals where they had granted to Winner's association, sole and exclusive rights as previously referenced. (Attachment 4) Since that letter, two (2) additional requests have been made to Winner to provide the subject agreement. None has been forthcoming.

Recently, the Association has provided certain players a letter dated December 13, 1996, (Attachment 5) in essence, dividing its membership into full members and associate members, depending upon when they played in the Negro Leagues, a copy of which is attached. We believe that Wilmer Fields is head of the Negro League Ballplayers Association and that the membership of the subject Association approximates between 50-70 former Negro League players which has not been substantiated.

109

Mr. Bud Selig
February 7, 1997
Page 4

In a desire, once and for all, for players who are still living to represent players and to truly develop programs for the best interests of the Negro League players, ~~Dennis Biddle and Sherwood Brewer~~ helped to form two (2) organizations. The first, Yesterday's Negro League Baseball Players, L.L.C., ("YNLBP") a Wisconsin limited liability company, (Attachment 6) was organized to:

1. The Association shall advance the public interest and the knowledge and understanding of the Negro Baseball League and its teams and players.

2. The Association shall seek enshrinement of all worthy members of the Negro Baseball League to the National Baseball Hall of Fame in Cooperstown, N.Y.

3. The Association will act as a spokesman for its members and represent its members with respect to any and all third-parties.

4. The Association will generate funds through sponsorship, licensing, autograph sessions and other forms of promotions to create a fund to benefit members in ill health and financial straits.

5. The Association, with the prior written consent of its members, shall utilize the names, images, signatures, autographs and likenesses of its members to promote the Negro Baseball League and its players with the purpose to generate income, which income, after the payment of expenses, shall be shared among the members.

The following persons were appointed as managers of YNLBP:

> Herman Doc Horn
> Verdell Lefty Mathis
> Robert Peach-Head Mitchell, Sr..
> Merle M. Fancy Dan Porter
> Herbert Harold Herb Briefcase Simpson
> Davey L. Wiz Whitney
> Jim Zipper Zapp
> William Fireball Beverly, now deceased
> Dennis Bose Biddle
> Sherwood Woody Brewer
> James Jimmy Dean Dean
> Melvin Buck Duncan
> Eugene Scruggs
> Cowan Bubba Hyde
> Joshua Josh Johnson
> Willie Bill Lee

109

Mr. Bud Selig
February 7, 1997
Page 5

The following were appointed Officers of YNLBP:

President	Sherwood Woody Brewer
President Elect	Dennis Bose Biddle
Secretary	Herman Doc Horn
Treasurer	Merle M. Fancy Dan Porter
Vice-President	Davey L. Wiz Whitney
Vice-President	Willie Bill Lee
Vice-President	Robert Peach-Head Mitchell

In addition to the limited liability company, Biddle and Sherwood also helped form Yesterday's Negro League Baseball Players Foundation, Inc., whose Board of Directors are Dennis Biddle, Verdell Lefty Mathis, William Beverly (now deceased), Sherwood Brewer, Herman Horn, Jr., and Merle Porter. (Attachment 7) The purposes of the Foundation are to preserve the history of the players that are currently living and who played in the Negro League through Hall of Fames, educational programs and other forms of perpetuation.

YNLBP currently has signed Membership Agreements of approximately one hundred eighty-one (181) members. Please find attached a list of those who have executed Membership Agreements. (Attachment 8)

Major League Baseball Properties has also been involved with the former players of the Negro League through a licensing program. However, the irony of Negro League licensing is that all team names, designs, trademarks and logos are the public domain, except those of the Monarchs, which the Museum bought from the team's last owner. Any company can produce goods without asking for license or paying royalties, a situation in contrast to the current day norm, in which sports leagues hold on tightly to licensing rights and get injunctive relief when those rights are infringed. Moneys generated from Major League Baseball Properties licensing are returned, in the form of checks, to players. Please find attached a letter dated July 29, 1996, relative to the last distribution. (Attachment 9) Please note that the distribution is not only to the former Negro League players, but also to the Negro League Museum and the Jackie Robinson Foundation.

We believe there are less than 300 living Negro League players. Larry Lester, the leading historian in the United States as it relates to the Negro League, has, through his research, made a list of who he believes to be the now living Negro League players. (Attachment 10)

As previously indicated, YNLBP represents, minimally, 181 of those players. It has been the continued position of YNLBP that the Negro League includes all of those players who played from the League's start in 1920 to the League's close in 1960. It is YNLBP's position that if a player played in the Negro League, the player should be benefited, regardless of longevity of their play and regardless of the fact that Jackie Robinson was admitted to the Major Leagues in 1947. YNLBP believes that although Jackie Robinson may have been admitted to the Major Leagues in 1947, the color lines were not eliminated and the Negro League continued to the League's end in 1960.

The Major Leagues have attempted, on several occasions, to benefit some, but few, of the Negro League players. On May 1, 1993, Major League Baseball introduced a new medical plan effective May 1, 1993, for former Negro League players and their wives. Although Major League Baseball would pay the full cost of the new medical plan coverage, few Negro League players knew of the proposed medical plan and, as a result therefore, did not sign up for the plan. It is my understanding that the medical plan has been closed out.

It should also be noted that at times, and throughout history, people associated with the Major Leagues have claimed to speak on behalf, and to represent the best interests of the Negro League. They include, current National League President, Len Coleman, and Vice-President of the Ballplayers Assistance Team (B.A.T.), Joe Black. Please be advised that although these gentlemen may have had the best interests of the Negro League at heart, the only organization that represents and speaks for the living players of the Negro League is the YNLBP.

Recently, it was announced that Major League Baseball has enacted a pension for players of the Negro League. It is our understanding that few living players will be included in the pension by virtue of the definition of eligibility. Once again, it is the YNLBP goal that all living players who played in the Negro League from 1920 to 1960, regardless of their longevity and regardless of Jackie Robinson's admittance into the Major Leagues in 1947, should be included and benefited by the pension plan.

It is YNLBP's purpose to obtain medical insurance and pension benefits from the Major League for all living members of the Negro League. Once again, we define the eligibility as those Negro League players, regardless of longevity, who played from 1920 to 1960 and regardless of the admittance of Jackie Robinson in the Major Leagues in 1947.

In May of this year, YNLBP will launch a national bus tour. The tour would include cities which have major league clubs. The bus tour will commemorate baseball and the Negro League Players. We would like Major Leagues, in conjunction to providing medical insurance and pensions, to honor these players as they take the bus tour of major league parks, similar to what was done in Milwaukee this past summer.

Commissioner, my clients would be happy to congregate in mass in Milwaukee, or any other place, to more vividly explain to you their plight and the needs of the current living players of the Negro League.

Thank you for your concern and any and all assistance.

Sincerely,

DEUTCH & GREENBERG

Martin J. Greenberg

MJG/mf
Enc.
cc: Mr. Dennis Biddle

A few weeks later, I received a telephone call from a reliable source that told me the grievance we filed created quite a stir in baseball. He told me that the criteria for the pension changed and that now about eighty-six people qualified for the pension. I was still wondering why YNLBP was not involved in any of the decision-making that affected its members so greatly. The caller also told me our grievance spurred the Major League Players Union to file their own grievance and that in turn caused the Major League's criteria for a pension to change as well. It now officially reads that only one day played in the major leagues is necessary to qualify for a pension.

A few days later, we received a letter from two promoters in Newark, NJ, inviting Mr. Brewer and me to an autograph session along with about eighty other Negro League ballplayers from around the country. I flew in to Newark from Salt Lake City. I was picked up at the airport and when I arrived at the hotel, I saw Buck O'Neil in the lobby. It was if he was waiting for my arrival. He all but ran over to me to tell that there was going to be a meeting after the autograph session because "the guys," he said, decided that they want an "older person" to run the organization that represents the players. I couldn't believe he was saying this to me! Three times before the meeting ever happened he told me how an older person should be put in charge of the foundation we had started.

110

THE NATIONAL PASTIME, INC.

145 HUGUENOT ST. SUITE 100 • NEW ROCHELLE, N. Y. 10801 •
(914) 576-2900 • FAX: (914) 576-2935
Harvey S. Brandwein, President   Stephen B. Hisler, Vice-President

June 1, 1997

Dear Negro Leagues Reunion Show Participant:

I would like to take this opportunity to thank you for participating in the 5th Negro Leagues Reunion Baseball Card and Memorabilia Show. This particular show is the longest continuous show of its kind and generally recognized as the biggest and best in the country. The first show was in May of 1992 and it has grown each year. This year more than 70 former Negro League players will be in attendance. The current show, as have the last three, is being sponsored in large part by Reggie Jackson. However, many others too numerous to mention have been instrumental in making this show successful. ***This package will include a schedule of events relating to the weekend, airline or train tickets where applicable, and all other information necessary.***

Date of Show: June 21 and June 22
Location: Meadowlands Hilton Hotel, Secaucus, New Jersey. Telephone number: (201) 348-6900
Ticket enclosed: Airline____✓____ Train_____ Not applicable_____
Arrival at Airport or Train Station: We will arrange to have someone meet you at the airport or train station. If you miss your pickup please take a cab to the hotel. You will be reimbursed for the cab.
Check-In At Hotel: When you check in at hotel, please see Barbara or Carmela from the National Pastime Staff. They can be found on the 2nd floor in Riverside Room 7 or 9. They will be there from 6-8 P. M. Friday. If your flights arrive after that time please see Jerry or Al in the Exhibition(attached to the Hotel) for your coupons. They will be presenting you with coupons to cover the cost of breakfast and dinner. These coupons will be presented only to the Negro League ballplayers. If you have friends or family visiting you, you can purchase additional coupons. The cost of the hotel room and taxes are of course taken care of. However, you will be responsible for all incidental charges.

Weekend events
Friday: No events. check in enjoy!
Saturday: Have breakfast at your leisure. ***Show hours***. Because of the large numbers of participants this year we have divided the signing into 2 sessions.

110

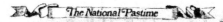

The National Pastime and Reggie Jackson *presents*

The 5th NEGRO LEAGUES REUNION SHOW

The largest gathering of former Negro League players ever assembled
as part of

THE MEADOWLANDS CLASSIC
A PREMIER BASEBALL CARD, MEMORABILIA, AND COLLECTIBLES SHOW
with the finest in cards, sets, rookie cards, autographs, memorabilia and collectibles

SAT & SUN	June 21 & 22	The Exhibition Center

SAT 9:00 AM - 5:00 PM
SUN. 9:30 AM - 4:00 PM
Free on site parking
for 2,000 cars.

The Meadowlands Hilton Hotel
2 Harmon Plaza
Secaucus, New Jersey
NJ Turnpike exit 16W to Rt. 3E
to Mead. Pkwy. Turn left.

STARRING (as of 4/1/97)
Tiant & Cepeda's fathers

Negro League & Major Leaguers   Mr. October   Negro Leaguer played in the Negro Leagues   HOFer

Monte Irvin	Joe Black	Sam Jethroe	Reggie Jackson	Buck O'Neil	Luis Tiant	Orlando Cepeda	Frank Robinson
Sat & Sun 11-2	Sat & Sun 11-2	Sat & Sun 11-2	Saturday only 12-3 Autographs	Sat & Sun 11-2	Sunday only 10:30-1	Sunday only 11:30-2	Sunday only 11:30-2
Auto: $15 bats $25	Auto: $10 bats $20	Auto $10 bats $20	flat items & balls $50 caps & equip $95. jerseys $125. bats $175	Auto: $10 bats $20	Auto $15 bats $25	Auto: $15 bats $25	Autogr. $25, caps & equ $45. 500 HR post $60. jers & bats $95

AND MORE THAN 50 FORMER PLAYERS FROM THE OLD NEGRO LEAGUES including former Major
Leaguers Bob Boyd, George Crowe, Chuck Harmon, J.C. Hartman, Pancho Herrera, John Kennedy, Jose Santiago & Ray Noble

Currently Scheduled Saturday and Sunday 11 am - 2 pm

Jimmy Armstead	Leroy Ferrell	James Ivory	Ray Noble
Russell Awkurd	Benny Felder	Pee Wee Jenkins	Ted 'D.D.' Radcliffe
Dennis Biddle	Josh Gibson Jr	Josh Johnson	Frazier Robinson
Gene Benson	Stanley Glenn	Mamie Johnson	Jim Robinson
Charlie Biot	Willie Grace	Larry Kimbrough	Joe B. Scott
Lyman Bostock Sr.	Nap Gulley	John Kennedy	Robert Scott
Bob Boyd	Chuck Harmon	Willie Lee	Eugene Scruggs
Sherwood Brewer	Willie Harris	Tony Lloyd	Jake Sanders
Jim Carter	Joe Henry	Max Manning	Jose Santiago
Gene Collins	Harold Hair	Enrique Maroto	Armando Vasquez
Leroy Cromartie	Raymond Haggins	Verdell Mathis	James 'Bo' Wallace
George Crowe	J. C. Hartman	Jim McCurine	'Curley' Williams
Jimmy Dean	Pancho Herrera (Sun)	Bobby Mitchell	Jim Zapp
Mahlon Duckett	Carl Holden	Jessie Mitchell	
Wilmer Fields	Doc Horn	Ira McKnight	

Autog. tickets for the Negro Leaguers are only $8 ea. A discount Superticket is available. Purchase 30 or more tickets and deduct $1.per ticket. Reggie Jackson will be donating his fee to the event. Frank Robinson will be donating a part of his fee to the event.

ADVANCE AUTOGRAPH TICKETS are available by mail or telephone for all guests. Please include a SASE with your order. You can also charge your tickets on Visa, Master Card, Discover, or American Express. A 5% postage, handling, and insurance fee will be added to all orders for tickets or mail order not accompanied by full payment.

To order advance tickets by phone, call our office
(9 1 4) 5 7 6 - 2 9 0 0 Monday - Friday 9am - 5pm.

ADMISSION IS ONLY $5 DAILY. A WEEKEND PASS IS ONLY $8

DEALER TABLES ARE $195 EACH, 2 for $360, 3 for $510

Send all requests for advance autograph tickets & dealer tables, to:

Send all requests for additional information to:

Stephen Hisler The National Pastime PO Box 604569 Bay Terrace Station Flushing, New York 11360 (718) 224-1795 after 5pm Office: M-F 9am - 5 pm (914) 576-2900	The National Pastime 145 Huguenot St. suite 100 New Rochelle, NY 10801 (914) 576-2900 fax (914) 576-2935

I found Mr. Brewer and I asked him if he knew anything about a meeting we were having here in Newark. Mr. Brewer said he did not but he did receive a letter about a meeting in Atlanta the following month. He asked if I received a letter about that meeting. I told him I had not and I told him about what Mr. O'Neil had been saying. Mr. Brewer questioned, "How can they take over something that we already started?" At that time, we both knew in our hearts that there was a set up taking place to oust me from the foundation so they could take it over, but why?

We knew that the major leagues had stopped the pension payments. Buck O'Neil and Joe Black knew that too. Perhaps the major leagues wanted to deal only with the organization that represented all of the players. That being the case, the only reason I could think of was that they wanted to be the ones in charge of representing us, but why? Perhaps it had something to do with the setting up of criteria so that any endowments or donations would only benefit older players. Perhaps it had to do with having control over any funds that might go to the players. I could only surmise. I told Mr. Brewer not to worry about it. I said the Lord will take care of it. And with that we went to the autograph signing session.

"I played with all these guys and for them to turn out like this, it's a disgrace. And especially Buck O'Neil. I am ashamed of them. So it's a gripe with me. I'm very bitter."
—Sherwood Brewer

After one of the sessions, Buck O'Neil called a meeting to order. I noticed Joe Black was in attendance too. Something told me this was not going to be just another friendly meeting. Mr. O'Neil said we were here because several organizations claim to represent the living players (Negro League Ballplayers Association and Yesterday's Negro League Baseball Players Foundation) and he wanted us all to get it straight once and for all.

Then Joe Black stood up and started to speak. He told us that the major league owners had put money up (we heard later it was about ten million dollars) to give us a pension, but it's been held up because a "little organization in Milwaukee" has got an attorney who knows the baseball Commissioner and they got it held up. He also said the major leagues owners are confused about who represents the players. This statement infuriated Mr. Brewer and me because we merely provided legal proof that our organization represented all of the players, not Len Coleman, the museum, Joe Black, Buck O'Neil, or any other organization. Obviously, they didn't like that we represented the players and now we knew why.

Unable to contain himself, Mr. Brewer stood up and asked,

"How can two people (meaning Black and Coleman) that's not even involved in any organization that represents us take over something that's supposed to go to us and set up criteria as to who's supposed to get it? It seems to me that they should have called on the organization (YNLBP) that represents the players."

Joe Black did not answer. He merely sat down. The crowd began to react loudly for Mr. Black to answer the question. Now other questions were being asked about who was eligible and how long the pension payments would be delayed. There was still no response. How could Mr.

Black respond? He was deeply involved in this and only eighty-six people qualified, according to their criteria, to receive that money! Now would be a very bad time for him to admit that.

As the crowd demanded answers from Black, Buck O'Neil stood up quickly and settled everyone down. We're gonna have a vote, he said. We're gonna have a vote as to what organization is going to represent the players. The first one we'll call on is the Ball Players Association.

The president of the Negro League Ball Players Association did not show up to the meeting so a representative stood up and talked about the things that the Association was doing for the older players. He talked about money that they had received that was already going to the older players.

That was not true because Mr. Brewer had been one of the oldest members and did not receive any money from them, as he should have. The spokesperson also stated that they were going to get a line of memorabilia and the proceeds from that would also go to all the older players. (Remember that during our investigation we found out that the Baseball Players Association only benefited, with few exceptions, the elderly former players who could travel to card shows. Remember too, allegations were made that some of the players were not being paid their royalties and that "certain personnel [had] converted money". Remember that we also found out that there was "no accountability with respect to funds generated" and "investigations" had been conducted "into the business of the organization by the District Attorney's Office of New York" (*New York Times,* March 15, 1993). Remember too, that even BAT had criticized the organization repeatedly.

Mr. Brewer, unable to listen to the deception any longer, hollered out, "Liar!"

At that time the speaker yelled back, "Shut up."

Mr. Brewer shouted back, "You don't tell me to shut up. Who do you think you are to tell me to shut up?"

It was clear that something physical was about to transpire so a few of us escorted a very heated Mr. Brewer out of the meeting. Then, after a few more comments, the speaker sat down. Buck O'Neil once again called for order. He then called on me to come up.

I took my briefcase and went up to the podium. I stood there a moment until the players settled down a bit more and then I spoke. "I am the president of Yesterday's Negro League Baseball Players Foundation. I represent all of you. Even if you didn't sign an affidavit, you are still covered by the Yesterday's Negro League Baseball Players Foundation because we represent all the living players of the Negro League Baseball. If you played in the Negro League, you are covered by our organization." I reached in my briefcase and took out a copy of an affidavit. "This was the affidavit that was sent to every living player," I said. "I only received one hundred eighty eight back. But even if you didn't fill out an affidavit you are still covered under the organization that represents you, the Yesterday's Negro League Baseball Players Foundation."

"Ladies and gentlemen," I continued, "Rube Foster is turning over in his grave right now. I can't believe this is happening the way it is. After finding out that we had no legal representation for our players, Mr. Brewer and I started this organization. If you look at the record, Yesterday's Negro League Baseball Players Foundation was filed before Negro League Ballplayers Association because the Negro League Baseball Players Association did not legally represent all the players. Therefore, we filed a charter for *all* the living Negro League ballplayers. Everyone is covered here, including the players who did not sign an affidavit. I did not file a charter for some of the players; I filed a charter for *all* of the players. Yesterday's Negro League Baseball Players Foundation represents *all* the players." I concluded and I sat down.

Buck O'Neil took the floor again and said we're gonna have a vote now on which organization will represent the players. Anyone who would like to have Negro League Baseball Players Association to represent the players hold your hand up. I saw one hand go up, the representative of the NLBPA.

When he asked who wanted the Yesterday's Negro League Baseball Players Foundation to represent the players, almost every person in the room raised their hand. At that time an ovation went out and Yesterday's Negro League Baseball Players was voted to represent the ball players. I looked around. Joe Black had his head in his lap as though he couldn't believe what had just happened. Buck O'Neil, who had presided at the meeting and who had told me that they wanted an older person running it, turned to me and said dejectedly, "Biddle, I will be sending in my application. He did so five years later.

Eleven more players asked me for applications, which I always carried in my briefcase. So now Joe Black knew for sure that we were the legal representatives of the living players of the Negro Leagues. Mr. Black could now go back to the major league owners and tell them that the decisions regarding the pension fund can go to the organization that represents the players. Buck O'Neil could also speak up on behalf of the organization that represents the ball players and take a stand.

Since I was not invited to the meeting in Atlanta, Mr. Brewer decided not to go either. I do not know exactly what occurred, but others told me that the meeting took place to once again try to vote me out of office. I surmised that since I did not attend the meeting, it was supposed to appear to the people at the meeting that I didn't care enough to come. That way, when they voted on who should be the president of the organization that represents them, they might not choose me. Since I am still president of the YNLBP, that didn't happen.

After the Atlanta meeting, I got another call from my friend telling me that the pension plan was now back in full swing. It now stood that anyone who played for the Negro Leagues and/or the major leagues for a total of four or more years would qualify for the pension. They added that at least two of those four years had to be played in the Negro Leagues. This change included eighty-seven people according to the new criteria set up. It would also include Mr. Sherwood Brewer. What this meant to me was that Black never went to the major leagues to tell them to go through us. He merely continued on with his scheme to keep control of the pension funds and distribute them as he saw fit.

It was no secret that Joe Black and Sherwood Brewer did not get along. Mr. Brewer was very outspoken about all former Negro League ballplayers. Mr. Brewer felt strongly that regardless of when a person played, a Negro League ball player was a Negro League ball player and should receive benefits and royalties as such. Black knew that Mr. Brewer and I had started an organization that would represent and benefit all the former players, including the younger ones who played after Jackie Robinson. Black belonged to an organization that benefited mostly older players that played before Jackie Robinson.

When pension checks were sent out to others but not to him, Sherwood Brewer was understandably upset. I found it to be especially disturbing because Joe Black played against Sherwood Brewer in the Negro Leagues, so he knew Mr. Brewer qualified. Joe Black also knew where Mr. Brewer lived because Mr. Brewer had been receiving assistance from BAT, the organization of which Mr. Black was vice president, so he couldn't claim the inability to find Mr. Brewer's address.

This was not the first time Mr. Brewer had difficulties because of Mr. Black. Several times in the past Mr. Brewer's assistance from BAT was mysteriously cut off. I had called BAT several times myself to let them know that Mr. Brewer had not received his assistance. The last time they cut him off I finally threatened them with legal action. It never happened again. Since Joe Black was vice president of BAT and since Mr. Brewer was outspoken about how he felt that every Negro League player should reap benefits, Mr. Brewer suspected that it was Black who cut off his assistance and purposely neglected to include him in the pension.

> "Mr. Brewer was an honest man, a man of principle. He stood his ground with what was real in the world as far as the haves and the have-nots. Until his dying day he held up the cause of equality regardless of Jackie Robinson. Jackie was an exception. He [Sherwood] stood firm in his belief that anyone one who touched the Negro Leagues, regardless of when, should be treated equally by major league baseball."
> —Martin Greenberg

I sent a letter to the baseball Commissioner along with the news article "Negro Leaguers to Get Pensions". I asked that he look into what had happened to the pension funds that were supposed to go to all the players. To this day, all Negro League ball players are not receiving the pension they deserve and to this day I have not received a response from the Commissioner regarding the issue.

> "We have brought to the attention of the Major Leagues the turmoil of what's going on in the office up there concerning us, the players. The headlines read Negro Leaguers to get pension, in big letters, but the way it was set up, very few of us will get the pension, and it's misleading. We want the public to know that there are two hundred fifty men still living out here. Most of them are poor."
> —Dennis Biddle

CHAPTER SIX
The Wall of Fame

I continued with my efforts to gain recognition for our foundation and to talk about our history. One day I was speaking at Jackie Robinson Middle School in Milwaukee, when a young lady asked if I would be a speaker at a program she was putting together for the Milwaukee Public Museum. I agreed and I spoke at the Milwaukee Public Museum during Black History Month about the Negro Baseball Leagues. I also talked about what I was doing to get recognition for the foundation and help for the living players.

A lot of questions were asked about the players that were still alive and the museum in Kansas City that was supposed to represent us. I explained the role of the museum and how it differed from the role of the foundation I had set up to represent the living players.

While speaking, I again was brainstorming about ways to get recognition for the living players of the Negro League. A thought came to me. What if I could get something in a major league park to honor the Negro Leagues? That way, we could get some true recognition. What if I could get something in every major league park? Then we would have recognition nationwide.

After speaking at the museum, I came up with an idea. I figured if we could get something in the Milwaukee County Stadium to represent and honor the living players from the Negro League, it might lead to getting something in other stadiums around the country.

I again went to the Brewers to ask for help. I met with Mr. Laurel Prieb who is the Vice President of Corporate Affairs to discuss the possibility of getting something having to do with the Negro League in the Milwaukee County Stadium. I wanted a special place in the stadium where we could honor living players from the Negro League for being such an important part of baseball history. It would be a permanent place with plaques on the wall and a place where we could induct different players each year.

He told me he would give it some thought. I told him that we don't have much time to think. These men were dying fast and we needed to do something now. Mr. Prieb asked me to put something in writing explaining what I had in mind.

I could write something up but I sure couldn't design what I had in mind. That day I happened to have lunch with the young lady who had brought me to the museum. We had discussed my idea before and I told her about my meeting with Mr. Prieb and what he wanted me to do. She said she would introduce me to Art Shea who was one of the curators of the Milwaukee Public Museum.

I met with him and since he knew nothing about the Negro Baseball League, I took thirty minutes to tell him about it and what has been happening to the living players. Then I told him about my plan to put something in the County Stadium to recognize the living players. He asked me to sketch what I had in mind on paper.

I went home and thought about what I wanted. I gave it some serious consideration. I then proceeded drawing a clumsy version of a "wall of fame". When I finished, I called Mr. Shea and immediately he asked me to bring it to him.

I presented my sketch of the wall of fame and how I thought it should look. Now, I am not a good artist but Art took the drawing nonetheless and said he would call me in a few days. He also kept my drawing and had it framed and put on his office wall!

About three days later he called me and asked me to meet with him. He showed me his rendition of the wall of fame that he had created based on my sketch. I looked at his drawing and became so excited that I called Mr. Preib to make an appointment with him as soon as possible. I wanted to show him this extraordinary design for our very own Yesterday's Negro Leagues Wall of Fame.

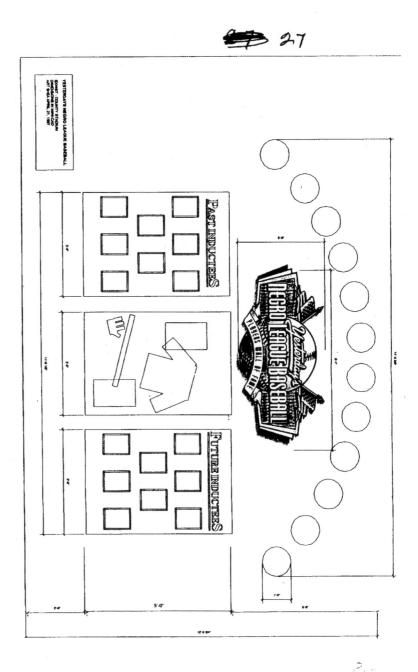

I took the drawing to the Milwaukee Brewers and met several times with Mr. Prieb. I explained about how important this wall was and how it would be good for the community. I explained how the wall would give fans a brief history of the men who played in the Negro Baseball Leagues.

Mr. Prieb took a copy of the plan and was very pleased with what he saw. Because Mr. Shea had included dimensions in his drawing, Mr. Prieb said he could look for a place to construct the wall and he would call me back.

In a few days, Mr. Prieb and I were walking around County Stadium looking for a space large enough to assemble the wall of fame. We found just the right place in the right field corridor of the stadium. Mr. Shea was then called in to see if what he was going to build would fit into the area designated for the Wall of Fame. It took awhile but Mr. Prieb finally okayed the project and Mr. Shea got to work.

After meeting with Art Shea on some specifics of how he wanted to build the wall and what it would take to build it, he gave me an estimated cost of what it would take to complete. The estimated cost would be $51,000.00. This number included a lot of pro bono work that Mr. Shea and others would contribute. I was flabbergasted at the cost.

Art Shea
Milwaukee Public Museum
800 West Wells Street
Milwaukee, WI 53233

26 FEB 1997

Marty Greenberg

Marty,

After meeting with Bennis Biddle and Terry Peterson at County Stadium, Emilio Bras (the lighting designer at the Museum) and I revised the budget for the project.

Phase 1 - Wall of Fame
3 Formica panels with Plexiglas box covers.
Title panel (Formica with vinyl application).
Vinyl title installation.
Photo mounting and installation.
Text layout and production.
Panel installation.
Lighting.
Rough estimate...18,900

Phase 2 - Miller Park
4 Formica bases with Plexiglas box covers.
Vinyl title installation.
Photo mounting and installation.
Artifact installation.
Mount making
Text layout and production.
Installation.
Lighting.
Rough estimate...32,600

Total...$51,500

If you have any other questions please call me at work.
My number at the museum is 278-6136. Thanks.

Art Shea

We had no money in the treasury. No cash donations were there yet. We certainly didn't have any cash to pay for the wall. The Brewers were giving us the space to display the wall at a Major League park and offered to donate the funds necessary to bring the players that were to be inducted that year to Milwaukee, so I felt that they had done enough. I was disappointed. I now had another obstacle to face. I had to figure out how to raise enough money to pay for this Wall of Fame. So Sherwood and I decided we would take to the streets, the airways and railways again, only this time asking for donations for the Wall.

During this time our attorney, Greenberg, introduced me to a friend of his named John Protiva. Mr. Protiva owned an insurance company and became very instrumental in helping us raise money for the wall. Since he had clients all over the city, he gave me a list of names and places to go to ask for donations. He told me to take my picture along and autograph it for anyone who donated. Money for the Wall finally started rolling in.

I raised about $8,000 through these efforts and I met a lot of good people. Even though I had $8000, it was nowhere near what I needed so I eventually went back to Mr. Shea to ask if he could possibly lower the cost of the Wall somehow. I was hoping he might be able to cut some corners somewhere to save us some money. Mr. Shea changed everything from the materials that the wall would be constructed of to the type of protective coating used. This time he was able to up with $18,000 as an estimate for the wall.

He was anxious to get started on the wall so I gave him the $8000 I had raised so he could buy some materials. He took the money and ordered the parts that needed to be paid for up front. This meant that the ball was rolling. It felt so good to know that something concrete was finally getting prepared to recognize these legends forever.

Then as fast as the donations had come, they had stopped. There were a lot of promises but no donations. We needed another $10,000 to pay for the other parts that Mr. Shea had ordered. We had one week left or the parts would have needed to be returned. This created a lot of sleepless nights for Mr. Brewer, Mr. Greenberg, and me. That feeling of helplessness came over me once again and once again, Mr. Brewer was there to reassure me. I am sure that the Milwaukee Brewers had no idea what we were going through to obtain the funds for this Wall of Fame.

Mr. Greenberg asked me about the stocks that Jimmy Dean had donated to us. We told him how we had turned the stocks around and invested them into Dean Whittier. Mr. Greenberg asked if we could borrow money against the stock. I had no idea so I called the broker and he said that the stocks were worth about $7500 and we could borrow as much as $4500 against the stock. Mr. Brewer and I went down and got the $4500 from Dean Whittier and took it back to Mr. Greenberg. We told him this was all we could get on the stock.

Mr. Greenberg then called his friend John Protiva again and told him he was sending us over to his office. We had no idea what else was said and no idea why we were to go there, but we trusted Mr. Greenberg and we went to Mr. Protiva's office.

Immediately upon arriving, Mr. Protiva called up Tri-City Bank, one block away from his office, and told the manager that he was sending us over to the bank. He instructed the manager to give us a cashier's check for $10,000 and to use the 100 shares of Merck stock as collateral for the loan. Then he told us to take our $4500 back to Dean Whittier.

We went to the bank, met with the manager and signed some paperwork to use our stock as collateral for the loan. We took the cashier's check and started walking back to Dean Whittier to take the money back. While in route, Mr. Brewer made the statement, " Here we are with $14,500 in my hand and we don't have a dime." We both chuckled at that.

After returning the money to Dean Whittier we met again with Art Shea and gave him the cashiers check so he could finish the Wall of Fame. With $18,000 from the foundation and some generous help from Martin Greenberg's friends, we were finally successful in making the Wall a reality.

Mr. Shea was able to finish the Wall. Within two weeks we had an unveiling ceremony and celebration at the Milwaukee County Stadium. It was so exciting. In the past, major league stadiums would stage Negro Leagues night each year and invite four or five players to honor that evening. They would give the former player a stipend and recognition for the evening but there was nothing concrete or permanent for players as a whole. The Wall of Fame gave us permanent recognition in a major league park and was endorsed by the acting Commissioner of Major League Baseball, Bud Selig.

Dennis "Bose" Biddle and Commissioner Bud Selig

Yesterday's Negro League Wall of Fame

Yesterday's Negro League Players Foundation President Dennis "Bose" Biddle

People who came to the stadium now had an opportunity to see and read about a part of American history that was never written down. Mr. Brewer and I made several visits to the stadium to view the beautiful Wall of Fame that we had created. It was amazing to me that we were actually able to make it a reality. One time we stood at a distance and watched the scores of people stop and study our Wall of Fame. We felt that we had finally started to get public recognition for Yesterday's Negro League baseball players. We were so very proud that we could accomplish this remarkable task. It was a feeling I will never forget.

The Wall of Fame flourished through generous donations from the Brewers and from autograph sessions we held with the inductees. Each year new players of the Negro League were to be inducted, provided they were still alive. The Brewers sponsored the inductees with transportation, hotel accommodations, a ceremony, and a stipend. In return, the inductees would sign autographs for fans during the game in which they were inducted.

" July 18th... the unveiling of the wall of fame...
To us it's big. It's the biggest thing that has ever happened to us. The world will get a chance to see the guys that are living today that made history in the Negro Baseball League. Not the guys that everybody talks about that has passed on."
—Dennis Biddle

"We think that people should know about this. We have ballplayers today who just flat out played that game. Some that people never heard of. Some that's good or better than the ones that they read about all the time."
—Sherwood Brewer

The plan was to induct nine people each year. Players such as Ernie Banks, Hank Aaron, and Mamie Johnson, the only living female Negro League player, were inducted. Even though we started with nine honorees, when the new stadium was built, things changed.

Our ultimate goal with the Wall was to educate the public about our history and to reveal the fact that there are still legends that played in the Negro Baseball Leagues alive today. We also wanted permanent acknowledgment in a major league park. The Wall symbolized that. We felt we were able to give living players recognition for being a part of the Negro Baseball Leagues.

WALL INDUCTEES

My aspiration now was to have a Wall of Fame for Yesterday's Negro Leagues in every major league park in the country. I hoped that since the Wall in Milwaukee was successful, other parks might come to us so I called several teams in the major leagues. One team responded with a request for a scaled-down version of the wall but it fell through in the process because they said it would be too expensive. Unfortunately, it was too costly for the foundation to put a Wall of Fame into all the major league parks around the country, and as we contacted other major league parks we were turned down every time. Worse yet, we were sometimes still not recognized as a legitimate organization! I felt as though we had hit another wall.

One day the Brewers called me and asked me what we planned to do with the Wall of Fame once everyone from the Negro League was gone. I thought about that. Then I remembered the scholarship program we set up. The way program, started in Wichita, operated was when a player passed, he would have a scholarship set up in his name in the city where he died. Since we had already given out two scholarships so far, we suggested that the recipients of the scholarship become the people to go on the Wall representing the Yesterday's Negro League Baseball Players Foundation. That would never happen.

It was at this time that the Brewers were getting ready to move into their new stadium and they decided to change our wall. They wanted to have a wall of honor there instead of a Negro Leagues wall. They told me that some parts of our wall would remain but not all. My heart sank as I thought of all the work and money we had put into making the Wall of Fame a reality and what would happen to the pieces they did not use. As always, the Lord was looking out for us.

It was Men's Day at Holy Redeemer Church of God and Christ, and the minister chose to honor me that year. The church also invited several other Negro League ball players, including Mamie Johnson, to join in the celebration. We went to watch the Brewers play, then and to the minister's home for dinner. He picked us up and dropped us off with first class service, limo and all. At dinner we were discussing what we should do with the left over pieces of the Wall of Fame once the new stadium was built. The minister suggested we might put them in the new building that had been built at his church. We all thought this was a great idea and we left with a renewed hope that we had a new home for the Wall of Fame once the new stadium was complete.

Later that year, Mr. Brewer and I were special guests at African World Festival. While autographing pictures for fans, a young lady approached us. She stated that she had found our Wall of Fame for sale on the Internet and that she had put in a bid. The closing bid, she added, would be Sunday, the next evening, at midnight. I was shocked by this news. No one had authorized the sale of our wall. This was being done without any knowledge or consent on our part. No one in the foundation had approved any part of our wall to be auctioned off! I immediately called our attorney, Mr. Greenberg, and told him about what was happening. He in turn called the Brewers and was able to stop the bidding on our Wall of Fame.

After four years of the Wall of Fame being in Milwaukee County Stadium, a replacement stadium was constructed. They changed our Wall and made it into a wall of honor instead. Now they only recognize two living Negro League players each year. The rest of the wall honors the Women's League (they recognize two per year) and Wisconsin players (they recognize two per year). This practice continues today.

Even though we spent a lot of time and money for our wall, I refused to be discouraged by this and busied myself with other avenues to continue to get recognition and benefits for the living players.

CHAPTER SEVEN
More Political Obstacles

Traveling was hard on Sherwood Brewer and me but we always pressed on. We were blessed to find the Motel 6. Their rooms were clean and their price was right. (We thank them for leaving the light on for us.) We also were blessed to have found Avis and rented a car. They kindly gave us a discount so we had a way to get around while traveling. It was also a blessing to have met so many interesting and influential people during our many engagements across the country. One couple in particular has helped our cause tremendously throughout the past few years.

While on a trip out west, Sherwood Brewer and Bobby Robinson had met a man named Sterling Ludlow and his wife, Thayes. They told the Ludlows about our organization and our cause. They explained to the Ludlows how the owners of the Negro Leagues did not preserve the name for the players who played in the League. They also explained how so many organizations have made a lot of money using the words Negro League and claim to represent the living players, yet the players actually reap little or none of the benefits of those sales. We told them how some of these organizations would even go so far as to say that the proceeds would be given to the living players, in order to make their sales, knowing full well that because the word Yesterday's was not in it, they were not bound to follow through with their promises.

The Ludlows were very interested in helping us expose our situation to the public if they could, so Mr. Brewer and Mr. Robinson asked them to give me a call. Because I was the main spokesman for the organization, they felt I would be a good person to contact. The Ludlows called and invited me to visit their home in Utah. They were very interested in what we had to say about the Negro Leagues and decided to help set up speaking engagements for me in their home state.

I spoke at a group home for troubled youth and on a subsequent visit, I spoke at Brigham Young University. I was also asked to speak at the University of Utah and at a high school commencement exercise in Spanish Fork, Utah.

After several trips, we were invited to set up a baseball workshop for kids in that area who wanted to participate in baseball. Not only was this workshop very successful, it gave us the chance to see our work having a positive impact on others in the community as well.

The Ludlows recognized that we needed help with our quest for recognition as a foundation and more importantly that we needed to educate the public about the word Yesterday's in our organization's name. Mr. Ludlow eventually approached us with an idea. He wanted to film a documentary. The documentary would be about the true history of the Negro League and what happened to the players who played in the Negro League from 1920 to1960. The documentary would reveal how the words Negro League, which was not preserved by the owners, have been working against the players that are living today. It would explain how players from the Negro League are still living today but our name and likeness are being taken advantage of by those seeking to gain from our hard work over the years. We felt the documentary was a wonderful idea and talked about how we might make it happen.

Mr. and Mrs. Ludlow knew we had no money so they offered to help raise money to film the documentary. Mr. Ludlow said he would help with fundraising and that he would ask a film crew he knew to film it. He also said he would help with the promotion of it after it was finished. He stated that the profits from the sale of the documentary, after expenses, would go to the foundation and to the players. Mr. Brewer and I were ecstatic. I couldn't believe that someone we hardly knew could be so good-hearted.

Excited and full of anticipation, I furnished all the information I could find to the people who were in charge of the documentary. When the director of the documentary interviewed Mr. Brewer and me he couldn't believe what he was hearing. He was surprised to hear what was happening, and not happening, to the Negro League players today. The people doing the filming were also really excited about the information we were sharing about the Negro Leagues. In order to reveal the plight of Yesterday's Negro Leagues, we knew we needed the valid testimony of other players as well, so we suggested a lot of players for them to interview to make it a worthwhile project.

One player interviewed was Frank Evans. He supplied quite a bit of information to help make the documentary. There were other players that we recommended to them that we felt would give useful information on the players of the League. For instance, they interviewed the only living female of the Negro League, Mamie "Peanut" Johnson. They also interviewed other former players about their experiences in the League and their experiences with other ball players. All of these people were members of Yesterday's Negro League Baseball Players Organization. The film crew even went to Chicago to interview some of the players that were not able to travel. Each time Mr. Brewer and I made trips to Utah to be interviewed on camera, we would bring other players with us to be interviewed as well. After awhile, the Ludlows became our friends. We enjoyed their company and I think they enjoyed ours. Sometimes they would bring us out there just to visit.

After what seemed like a long time, a ten-minute starter was finally finished. Even though the documentary was started, it had many setbacks. The reason for most of the setbacks was because the documentary was made to reveal the word Yesterday's, and how it represented *all* living players, whether they signed an affidavit or not. Since other organizations were still claiming to represent us, they kept contacting the Ludlows about that word, Yesterday's—they did not want that word in there. If Yesterday's Negro League Ball Players were the beneficiary of the profits from the documentary, then ONLY the living players would benefit from the documentary and no other organizations. Fortunately for us, the Ludlows were only interested in the living players and their well-being and not some faceless corporation's success, so they refused to change their mind.

CHAPTER EIGHT
A Tribute To The Past

One day, I was signing autographs at Lackland Air Force Base in Texas, trying to make money for the foundation. As I spoke about the history of the Negro League and how I was trying to get benefits for the living players, a young lady was standing at the end of a table listening intently. The next day, the same lady approached me and said that the Lord had come to her and told her to write a play about the true history of the Negro League. Her name was Joyce Christopher. She asked me if she could write a play based on what I had said the day before. Now being a man of means, I felt that any way we could get the word our about who we are and what we are trying to do would be a positive step so I agreed and I told her that I would give her any information she would need to write the play.

We talked almost every day and I sent information to her about the League and me. It was five or six months later when she presented me with a transcript of a play that represented everything that I had been doing (and had done) to try to keep Yesterday's Negro League alive. It was amazing to me how she put together something that was so true. She never knew my mother or my father, or my sisters or brothers but the way she wrote the play brought tears to my eyes because it had brought back those memories of what had happened in my life and how I got where I was today. It was so real it was uncanny. She named the play, *Yesterday's Dream Alive.*

Once I approved the script, we talked every day on how we could present the play to the world and eventually we became very good friends. We put ads in the Austin paper in hopes of getting actors for the play. Within no time she had a partial cast together. It seemed however, that every time an actor would agree to be in it, they were excited at first but soon lost interest. Joyce would just say to me, "The Lord didn't intend for this to be." And then she would say, "When the right one comes along, the Lord will let us know." We ran many ads in the paper looking for actors. One day she called me and told me that she had finally found someone to play my mother. She sounded very relieved because apparently she wanted to find just the right person to play the part.

One by one she found actors to play my sisters and my brothers. Finally a cast was put together and rehearsals began. She did not want to start this play with me as an adult. She wanted to start it when I was younger. She wanted to play out on stage how I got started in the Negro League and how and why I started the foundation. She felt that this was a good way of getting the true history to the people that knew nothing about the Negro Baseball League. She also felt that it was a good way to let people know what has happened to the players that are still living today. I agreed.

Her husband, who was in the military, was transferred to Del Rio, Texas, during this time and this meant that Joyce would have to travel hundreds of miles each week to get to rehearsal. I became very concerned about the viability of the play. The move had caused a lot of wear and tear on Joyce and on her automobile but she would always say, "I'm doing the will of God." This was encouraging to me because it alleviated a lot of the pressure I was feeling about the play and it enabled me concentrate on the other things I was doing to get recognition for the foundation. I turned the play over to her completely and she in turn notified me of what was happening with it on a continual basis.

On August 10, 2002, we opened the play at the Market House Theatre in Paducah, Kentucky, during our second annual convention. We felt this was a good time to introduce to the world, acted out on stage, the true history of Yesterday's Negro Baseball League. I remember sitting there watching the play with tears in my eyes because it was so real to me. I can't put it into words. She put it together like it really was my childhood, my going to the Negro League, and the things that happened in the Negro League. She just put it all together so well.

The play is still ongoing and we put the transcript in the hands of screenwriters to possibly make it into a movie. I don't know what will happen with that, but I will always hope for the best and keep pushing forward.

CHAPTER NINE
Helpful Support

Along with the other fine people I met during my travels and my trials with the foundation, I met a gentleman by the name of Robert Pyles. Mr. Pyles owned five McDonald's in the Milwaukee area and seemed to show an interest in the history of the Negro Baseball League. One day he approached me about the possibility of putting some of our history in one of his stores. I was eager to talk with him about the offer and after several meetings with him, he decided to make one of his stores an All-Sports McDonald's. It would not only have the history of the Negro Baseball League in it, but it would have other sports represented as well.

I was told that I could display the complete history of the Negro Baseball Leagues if I wanted. That was an offer I couldn't refuse. This was an opportunity that could last for a long time. When our young people came to this McDonald's, they would have an opportunity to see and learn about the history of Negro Baseball. I was tickled to be a part of his plan and have made it a point to endorse his store. I made many appearances at that McDonald's to promote the displays of our history, signing autographs, along with several other players, and talking about the history of the Negro Baseball League. It took thousands of dollars to put this All-Sports McDonald's together and I am appreciative for the opportunity to display our history within its walls today. I am also eternally grateful for all of the additional help Mr. Pyles has given to the foundation and our members throughout these years. If it weren't for Mr. Pyles, we would never have been able to have our foundation's first reunion.

Our first reunion took place in Bossier City, Louisiana, and it is a miracle it happened at all. It began when I was signing autographs at a shopping mall in Bossier City. A young lady approached me about having a Negro League event where she worked at a casino called Isle of Capri. She stated that the casino might help sponsor an event and she would work with me to make it happen. I was all for the idea.

After working so hard for the past few years trying to get the foundation set up, I thought it would be nice to be able to bring the members of Yesterday's foundation together for a reunion, so we talked daily on how to set up an event that would serve as a reunion for us. She said she would work on getting the casino to help sponsor the event and I should work on making sure all of the players got to Bossier City for the event. Now, getting everyone there would be tricky because a lot of these people had little disposable income to spend hopping on a plane and traveling to another state just to get together.

The casino agreed to help sponsor the reunion and furnished hotel accommodations and food for the players. The rest of the program was set up through local churches and the local Minor League baseball club in the city. Unfortunately, I was having some serious problems getting my part of the job done.

Because some of the players lived in the area, we decided that those players who could would drive to the reunion. Other players would need to fly. After trying to get money raised for airfare, it looked as though we wouldn't be able to pull it off, so I called players that I knew could afford to pay for their travel, which was about twelve to eighteen players, and they agreed to pay their own way. We knew then that even though small, we would still have a gathering. The next thing I did was call various organizations and ask them for donations to fly the rest of the players in. Each time I asked I was turned down. Asking for help had seemed to become such an integral part of my life that it was no longer as difficult as it used to be. I know that I am asking for a good cause and believing in my cause makes it much easier. I no longer feel the rejection that I used to when I began my quest but it was always a let down when people said no and this time I was feeling quite let down.

During a meeting with Mr. Pyles regarding the All Sports McDonald's, he asked me why was I looking so sad. I told him that we were supposed to have a reunion and I didn't have the money to fly all of the guys in. He asked me how much money I needed. I gave him my best guess and he wrote me out a check for five hundred dollars more than I had told him! It was a godsend. I thanked him and went straight to the airport with a list of players to be flown to Bossier City for our reunion. It was exciting and gave me renewed hope.

Even though the money had brought a lot of players in, it wasn't enough to bring them all. We still had about ten players we couldn't afford to bring and I was determined to find a way to bring them. I just didn't know how I would do it yet.

The next morning, Mr. Pyles and I were at the corporate office of McDonald's in Milwaukee. Mr. Pyles explained to his district manager what was happening and the District Manager asked me how many more players we needed to sponsor. I told him and he told his secretary to get a list of those players and make flight plans to get them to Bossier city. I was both elated and in disbelief at the same time. God had sent me the help I needed time after time and here it was again. I happily gave her a list of names. Now those ten players who would not have been able to attend were coming, thanks to the District Manager of McDonald's and Mr. Robert Pyles.

The reunion was really a tear jerker. Players hadn't seen each other for a long time and were finally together again. There were eighty-five of us, and it was a glorious three days. We went to schools and churches to speak and we were guests at the local ballgame. The casino sponsored a banquet for us and everybody had a glorious time. During that weekend several players approached me and asked how I managed to get this together and my reply to each of them was, "By the grace of God."

We thought it would be a great idea to have a reunion every year at the Bossier City Casino but we were disappointed when the management of the casino said that they would not be able to sponsor such an event annually due to other casinos moving into the area thereby affecting their revenue. This was a minor setback but by now I was beginning to get used to those.

CHAPTER TEN
For The Young

I was awakened one night by something that had been on my mind for several days. I wanted to leave something behind for my young people so they can always refer to it for important dates, special events, birthdays, and even deaths of the players of the Negro Baseball League. Many nights were spent thinking about what I could do. Then I finally put it together. I thought about making a collectible calendar. Put together with the affidavits of the players, information from reliable books, stories from the players themselves, and the history that was handed down to me through the years, I felt that these calendars would represent us well. I figured that five volumes would just about cover everyone and everything that has happened. This would be something that would be a reference young people could use throughout their lives about a part of history that even their mother or father could not communicate to them.

After putting my thoughts together about what I wanted in volume one, I presented my idea to a young lady who said she would work with me to get this together right away. I gave her a lot of important information including books, documents, and papers she would need to complete volume one on time for production. I met with her several times but then never heard back from her so I was forced to continue with the project on my own. I was on a tight time schedule and although I was now without help, it was too important to let go. I was able to get it completed on my own but it was quite some time later when I was finally able to reclaim my materials through a mutual friend.

After I completed volume one, I went to a graphic company and they gave me a price I couldn't afford even though I did the whole layout myself. Again I solicited several organizations asking for help in printing the calendar and once again I was turned down. I knew I could generate some money with autograph signings but not that much in a short amount of time.

Eventually I went back to the All-Sports McDonald's to speak with Robert Pyles and ask him for help with my calendar. Five hundred calendars would cost $1,400 and I needed help coming up with the money. Mr. Pyles generously gave me enough to cover half the cost of the calendars and I was able to sign autographs to pay for the other half. Now we have something that I feel is very important for my young Americans. I purposely set it up so that even if someone were missing a volume of the calendar they would be able to call the foundation and get whatever volume they needed. I felt this was another milestone met in my endeavor for historical recognition for the Negro League.

CHAPTER ELEVEN
A Precious Gift

As we fought to resolve the insurance and pension issues of the Negro League with the Major League, I continued to travel throughout the United States sharing our history and gaining recognition for our foundation. It was a battle worth fighting because even if I lost the war, I knew that at the very least the Negro Leagues would never die completely. Even when all of us old men pass away, I will have shared our history for the next generation to pass on and I will have left a legacy, no matter how small, to help people remember us. In the meantime, I was always brainstorming about ways to make money for the foundation.

One day I came up with an idea to generate some funds for the foundation. Since I had access to all of the former Negro League players, I thought I could have a quilt made with the autographs of every living player of the Negro Baseball Leagues. I figured we could auction it off to generate some revenue for the foundation. I went and bought material and cut it into five by five-inch squares.

I decided that I should make five of these quilts. I autographed five pieces of the material and had Mr. Brewer autograph five pieces as well. Hundreds more players and other celebrities I met signed material for me too. At this point I have many autographs of famous people I had met that make up the sports world, and I got a few movie stars too. I even got the autograph of one of the Munchkins from the original 1939 movie *The Wizard of Oz*. The first quilt is currently in production by a wonderful woman in Las Vegas who offered to donate her time and talent to our cause. This first quilt should be ready for auction within a short time.

CHAPTER TWELVE
The Ultimate Resolution – February 27, 2002

After learning about the Negro Baseball Leagues and the fact that the major leagues never formally apologized for what had happened to the players, US Representative J. C. Watts (R-Oklahoma) wanted to present a resolution before Congress honoring the players and the teams that made up the Negro Baseball League (1920-1960). This resolution will be in history books and will be a document that admits, as the United States of America, that Blacks were left out of the major leagues and all that it represents. It would be fifty years late, but thank God, it has finally happened. I wish the major league could see the long-term affects their decisions, even back then, have had on the former players of the Negro Leagues. In any case, the United States of America was finally recognizing us and I felt it would be a great opportunity to expose the nation to our foundation and our cause.

When a person representing Watts called me asking for my presence at the reading of the resolution, I eagerly accepted the invitation. I called to make sure they knew that Yesterday's Negro League Baseball Players Foundation represented the living players and I sent them legal documents to that effect, along with a current list of players. A short time later I received a formal letter requesting my presence when congress made the resolution in Washington.

101

107TH CONGRESS
2D SESSION

H. CON. RES. 337

Recognizing the teams and players of the Negro Baseball Leagues for their achievements, dedication, sacrifices, and contributions to baseball and the Nation.

IN THE HOUSE OF REPRESENTATIVES

February 27, 2002

Mr. Watts of Oklahoma (for himself and Mr. Davis of Illinois) submitted the following concurrent resolution; which was referred to the Committee on Government Reform.

CONCURRENT RESOLUTION

Recognizing the teams and players of the Negro Baseball Leagues for their achievements, dedication, sacrifices, and contributions to baseball and the Nation.

Whereas even though African-Americans were excluded from playing in the major leagues of baseball with their Caucasian counterparts, the desire of some African-Americans to play baseball could not be repressed;

Whereas African-Americans began organizing their own professional baseball teams in 1885;

Whereas 6 separate baseball leagues, known collectively as the Negro Baseball Leagues, were organized by African-Americans between 1920 and 1960;

Whereas the Negro Baseball Leagues included exceptionally talented players;

Whereas Jackie Robinson, whose career began in the Negro Baseball Leagues, was named Rookie of the Year in 1947 and subsequently led the Brooklyn Dodgers to 6 National League pennants and a World Series championship;

Whereas by achieving success on the baseball field, African-American baseball players helped break down color barriers and integrate African-Americans into all aspects of society in the United States;

Whereas during World War II, more than 50 Negro Baseball League players served in the Armed Forces of the United States;

Whereas during an era of sexism and gender barriers, 3 women played in the Negro Baseball Leagues;

Whereas the Negro Baseball Leagues helped teach the people of the United States that what matters most is not the color of a person's skin, but the content of that person's character and the measure of that person's skills and abilities;

Whereas only in recent years has the history of the Negro Baseball Leagues begun receiving the recognition that it deserves; and

Whereas baseball is the national pastime and reflects the history of the Nation: Now, therefore, be it

Resolved by the House of Representatives (the Senate concurring). That Congress recognizes the teams and players of the Negro Baseball Leagues for their achievements, dedication, sacrifices, and contributions to baseball and the Nation.

Website: www.ynlbpc.com

122

◁ A MESSAGE FROM HOUSE REPUBLICAN ▷ CONFERENCE CHAIRMAN J. C. WATTS, JR.

J.C. WATTS, JR.
4TH DISTRICT, OKLAHOMA

CHAIRMAN,
HOUSE REPUBLICAN CONFERENCE

COMMITTEES
ARMED SERVICES
SUBCOMMITTEE ON MILITARY PERSONNEL
SUBCOMMITTEE ON MILITARY PROCUREMENT
PANEL ON MORALE,
WELFARE AND RECREATION

OFFICES:
1007 LONGWORTH BUILDING
WASHINGTON, DC 20515
(202) 225-6165

2420 SPRINGER DRIVE
SUITE 120
NORMAN, OK 73069
(405) 329-6500

WICHITA NATIONAL LIFE BLDG.
711 S.W. D AVENUE, SUITE 201
LAWTON, OK 73501
(580) 357-2131

Congress of the United States
House of Representatives
Washington, DC 20515–3604

September 18, 2002

Dear Negro League Veterans:

I would like to welcome you all to this historic event recognizing your accomplishments as professional baseball players and members of the Negro Baseball Leagues, but more importantly recognizing your dedication, sacrifices and contributions to this Nation. It is an honor to be among such dedicated men and women who played such a significant part in making some of sports history's greatest moments.

Since 1885, with the love for the game in their hearts, African-Americans began to organize their own professional baseball teams in response to the segregated society of the times, which excluded them from playing in the major leagues of baseball with their counterparts. For decades men like those of you here today sacrificed and committed their time and effort to breaking the color barrier that for too long determined which men, according to the color of their skin, were afforded the opportunity to realize their dreams.

Today, although many have heard of Negro Leagues Baseball, few comprehend the magnitude of its impact on not just the game of baseball, but also on our society.

Today, I am privileged to join Congressmen Danny Davis and Charles Rangel and Senators Rick Santorum and Barbara Mikulski, our celebrity guests and all of the sponsors for today's event in saying thank you. I appreciate your commitment, determination and your persistence to fulfilling not just your individual dreams but also the dreams of a nation of people who aspired to pursue the vision of our founding fathers: life, liberty and the pursuit of happiness.

Sincerely,

Rep. J.C. Watts, Jr

◁ 3 ▷

We were brought to Washington D.C. from all over – Chicago, Birmingham, Tampa, Alabama, and other places from around the country. Former players from the Kansas City Monarchs, the Indianapolis Clowns, the Birmingham Black Barons, and the Chicago American Giants were there. Some of us flew there, but most of us came via Greyhound, since the bus line was a sponsor. These buses were real nice. They even had bathrooms! I remember when I was playing ball, we had to pull over and go in the woods.

And with our baseball caps on and our hearts warm with pride, we slowly stepped off the buses. We climbed those steps of the Thomas Jefferson Building in Washington D.C. and we all met in the Library of Congress and reminisced. We savored the moment as we do every time we are together. We know deep down that each time we meet, it may very well be the last time we will see each other.

Congressman J.C. Watts was our host for the event. Earlier in the day, he introduced a resolution in the House honoring the contributions of those who played in the Negro Leagues. A similar resolution was introduced in the Senate. He started the event by thanking us for coming. "You persevered under unimaginable hardships," Watts said when he addressed us. He called us national treasures. Our country was finally recognizing us and we finally felt the proper recognition for which we had been waiting.

There were about sixty-five of us there to hear the resolution. We'd lost quite a few players since our 75th reunion. Sherwood Brewer got up at one point and rattled off the names of his teammates and friends who had died just in the last year or so. "We're down to about one hundred and eighty men," he said. Ted "Double Duty" Ratcliff was there too. He turned one hundred that July.

We had lunch and listened to speeches and presentations. It took almost two hours but the time seemed to fly by. At one point they played the national anthem and we all sung in unison. Then we all yelled, "Play ball!" It was really a great time for us.

Rev. William Greason, who played for the Black Barons, gave an invocation thanking the Lord for us saying, "Oh, Lord, we thank you for these Negro Leaguers." Celebrity lawyer Johnnie Cochran, gospel performer MC Hammer, and actor Blair Underwood all came to honor us too. Underwood said, "Today, your country remembers you, and you will never be forgotten." Underwood's uncle, Eli, had played for the Negro League baseball team in Pittsburgh.

Tears came to my eyes often that day. Then Buck O'Neil stepped up to the microphone and said, "You don't have to feel sorry for these guys. They played with some of the greatest athletes ever." And then Willie Mayes cried. And he should have.

A couple of weeks before this event, when Watts called Mayes to invite him, Mayes had never even heard of him. Even though Mayes had spent three seasons with the Black Barons as a teenager before going to the New York Giants in 1951, he was never active in any Negro League functions. Maybe he just wanted to forget. Anyway, when he understood the magnitude of what would be taking place on Capitol Hill, Mayes told Watts he would be there.

Willie Mayes got up with a tear and spoke. For the first time in public, Willie Mayes admitted that we were the players that made it possible for him to be in the major leagues. He recalled that the older players on his team clearly knew that he would make it to the majors. They knew they were too old and couldn't make it but they always encouraged Mayes. "You can make it," Mayes recalled them saying to him. "I've never forgotten that. They might think I did, but I didn't. This is why I'm here." "So guys, thank you. Thank you very much." Tears rolled down his cheeks.

When the resolution was finally read we all became emotional. This was the moment for which we had waited fifty years. Washington D.C. honored us on behalf of the nation. The resolution acknowledged the wrongs that were done to us so long ago, the wrongs that still affected so many of our lives today. We are still waiting for the major league to give a formal repentance for what happened to the Negro League players but based on their actions thus far, we expect it will probably never happen.

Although we all went home with a sense of pride and renewed hope, most of us still didn't have a pension or the medical insurance, which was offered by the major leagues.

CHAPTER THIRTEEN
No Bats Go To Bat

In 2002, Joe Black died. Len Coleman's job was eliminated as president of the National League in that same year. We felt that if anything were going to change for us, now would be the time.

There had been many organizations that have approached me wanting to help the living players but few ever followed through, so when I was contacted by an organization called the No Bats Baseball Team, I had no reason to believe this organization would be any different.

Dennis "Bose" Biddle and Hall of Fame Nolan Ryan

A man on the telephone introduced himself as Ted. He explained to me that their organization was a group of businessmen, all former amateur baseball players, who put together an annual fundraiser to benefit charitable organizations. He told me that he had contacted the Negro League Museum in Kansas City about helping the ball players but they told him that they no longer represented any of the players. He told the museum that his organization wanted to help the players and that is how he got my telephone number.

I told him about our organization and that we represented all of the living players of the Negro League. He told me that they were going to have a fundraiser in August and he would like the proceeds to go to our organization. He also asked me to give him the names of ten players that may need help right away, those who had medical issues or had other difficulties. Since I did not know all of the players personally, I relied on the player that did know them—my comrade, Sherwood Brewer. Mr. Brewer gave me a list of eight players that he knew of who were in dire need of help and I forwarded those names to Ted.

The next day, the sister of a former Negro League player contacted me. She called me crying because her brother had recently passed away and she didn't have any money to give him a burial. His body had been at the funeral home for more than a week. She asked if the organization could help out in any way. Since we had little money, I decided I would ask some of the other living players to donate money to help bury one of our brothers. As I was getting a list of names together to call for help, I got another call from Ted. I told him what had happened and what I was going to do.

He asked me where the player lived and to give him the name of the funeral home where he lay. I gave him the name of the funeral home and the telephone number of the man's sister.

Ted's organization contacted the funeral home and took care of all of the burial arrangements for our fallen brother. This made me realize that this organization was for real. I was grateful to God that my prayers had been answered. We finally found an organization that recognized our foundation as legitimate, that understood what we are trying to do, and that was willing to help us.

After many conversations with Ted and his counterpart, JJ, about our organization, what happened in the past, and what was supposed to happen but didn't (regarding the medical insurance and pension), they understood what we were trying to accomplish. They asked me to send them legal documentation of our organization and of everything I could find having to do with our efforts with the major leagues medical insurance and pension issues. They also asked for a complete list of names of the living players.

I supplied them with the information they had asked for and then they said they would look into the situation. In the meantime, I was comforted to know that some very generous and caring people were tending to some of the desperate needs of our former players.

After a few days, JJ called me to say he could not get any information from the Major League. That didn't surprise me. I made a few calls and was able to get the phone number of the department in the Major League that was in charge of sending out the pension checks. I turned that telephone number over to JJ at No Bats and once again he said they would follow up on the situation.

No Bats called me again a few weeks later. They told me they were getting a lot of calls from other organizations complaining that they represented the living Negro League ballplayers and that No Bats should help them instead. No Bats, as did a lot of other people trying to help us in the past, including the major leagues, did not want to get in the middle of what seemed to be an ongoing political dispute between the Negro League ball players and who legitimately represented them.

It is so sad that after all the meetings and the voting we did in these past eight years, some of the ball players and other outside organizations are still trying to take control of what we legally started. If only we could stand as one, we could accomplish so much, but it seems there will continue to be those who will try to get money funneled in their direction for their own selfish intentions.

"The problem with the Negro League is that they did not group together as one. There are too many divisions and jealousy to give the group, as a whole, strength. There are too many self-interests preventing them, as a group, to portray their image and take advantage of a means to market themselves."
—Martin Greenberg

Ted called and told me they decided to meet with BAT since it is a recognized organization that is responsible for helping former major league and Negro League ball players. Although they said nothing to me about the medical insurance or the pension issue at this time, it was obvious that No Bats wanted to help us and I didn't mind if they went through BAT, now that Joe Black was gone.

The No Bats organization met with BAT and gave them the information we supplied including our list of all former Negro League players. No Bats told me that they would donate money from their fundraising efforts to us through BAT. Now if any of our members need help and want it, (for anything from living expenses to medical expenses) they can get it though B.A.T. if their name is on the list. I was elated!

It is important to note that Yesterday's Negro League Baseball Players Foundation exists to help the players, and even though the money No Bats is donating to us goes through BAT, Joe Black and Len Coleman have no more control in the matter, so we are comfortable knowing that the money will really come to all the Negro League players who need it, not just a select few.

Although most players still don't have the Major League medical insurance, another milestone had been reached because help for medical expenses is now available to all of us if needed. No Bats also mentioned to me that they are now going to focus on the pension issue.

There will be no more worrying about meeting the unrealistic criteria or guidelines that Joe Black and Len Coleman set up in the past. There will be no more mysterious list that contains only a fraction of the players of the Negro Leagues. The only criteria necessary to receive these benefits is that you played in the Negro Leagues between 1920 and 1960, just as we had voted on at our 75th reunion back in 1995.

"Joe Black only wanted to help those former Negro League players he felt deserved it and he made that happen through his controlling powers when he worked for BAT. I remember asking Black for medical insurance applications back in the beginning to help everyone. Black refused. And he refused to step in to get everyone a pension that they deserved and he covered his hidden agenda with unreasonable guidelines. There was a lot of money that was given with the intention of all Negro League players receiving something and it was not going where it needed to go. Even though Joe Black is gone, those guidelines are still in there and no one is saying why. I still wonder about the medical insurance offered to all of us. I still hope for a Major League pension some day."
—Dennis Biddle

The people responsible for supplying a list of eligible players did not supply a list that reflected all of the players. A complete list of names of the living players was given to Bud Selig by Mr. Brewer and me. Selig said he would pass this list on to all the owners of the major league ball teams but to this day we have heard no confirmation that they received the documents. I felt that the two men in the major league office who were responsible for setting up the criteria for who would get the money were partial. Because of personal feelings many players did not receive the money. We had the complete list of the players but they didn't want it. If the major league had come to the foundation that represented all the players, we could have worked with them to get the money to them. Some of the players who have died would have had received some kind of benefits before they died. But because of greed, most of the players that are living today receive nothing. This is by no fault of the major leagues. They relied on these two individuals to be fair and to be competent. But they found only a few and then decided to close out the offer. If Faye Vincent ordered this, who ordered that it be done in only six months? These guys lived all over the country! No one could find all of them in only six months. A few years later, in 1996 when I found this out and called them to inform them that I found the rest of the guys, he hung up the telephone on me. Faye Vincent was no longer commissioner. Selig got rid of Len Coleman but we still feel that *all* the players deserve medical and a pension.

The no bats went to bat for us and got a hit!"

—Dennis Biddle